mlr
Marxist Left Review

Number 29 – Winter 2025

Editor
Omar Hassan

Editorial committee
Mick Armstrong
Sandra Bloodworth
Omar Hassan
Louise O'Shea
Jordan Humphreys

Reviews editor
Alexis Vassiley

© Social Research Institute

Published by Socialist Alternative
Melbourne, August 2025

PO Box 4354
Melbourne University, VIC 3052

www.marxistleftreview.org

marxistleftreview@gmail.com

Contributions to *Marxist Left Review* are peer-reviewed

ISSN 1838-2932
rrp. $20

Subediting and proofreading
Tess Lee Ack
Diane Fieldes

Layout and production
Susan Miller
Luka Kiernan

Printed by IngramSpark

Marxist Left Review is a theoretical journal published twice-yearly by Socialist Alternative, a revolutionary organisation based in Australia.

We aim to engage with theoretical and political debates on the Australian and international left, making a rigorous yet accessible case for Marxist politics. We also seek to provide analysis of the social, political and economic dynamics shaping Australian capitalism.

Unless indicated otherwise all articles published reflect the views of the individual author(s).

We rely on our readers' support to continue publication.
You can help by subscribing at
marxistleftreview.org

mlr
Marxist Left Review

Number 29 – Winter 2025

OMAR HASSAN

Trump ushers in a more barbaric capitalism

Omar Hassan is an editor of *Marxist Left Review*. He is a long-term activist in anti-fascist and Palestine solidarity work and has written extensively on the Middle East.

T RUMP'S fiRST SIX months have dramatically transformed both US and global politics. His return to the highest office in the land was foreshadowed for some months, with the hapless figures of Biden and Harris incapable of staving off the resurrection of one the most incoherent, incompetent – and yet dangerously fascistic – figures in history.

Trump immediately declared that he had a "massive" mandate to radically restructure the politics, international relations and economics of the US, and as a result, the world. Trump's first presidency was a surprise even to Trump, but this time he meant business. His supporters had developed a broad plan, known as Project 2025, to make US capitalism more authoritarian and pro-business than ever before. As well, without overstating their coherence, his team seemed more serious than last time round, and together enjoyed the fairly disciplined support of nearly the entire Republican party.

Trump began his reign with a bang, unleashing 26 reactionary executive orders in his first day in the Oval Office. Eventually a record 142 orders were signed in the first 100 days, an unprecedented onslaught against workers and the oppressed. The most publicised of these have involved dramatic attacks on women, LBGT, refugee and migrant communities. These include abolishing all programs designed to provide some assistance to oppressed minorities in employment, education and society, given the umbrella term of Diversity, Equity and Inclusion (DEI). While some of these measures are entirely token and cynical, Trump's move also undoes some of the more substantial gains won during the civil rights era. His declaration of war on the trans community is breathtaking in its scope, including expelling them from the US army, the federalisation of bans on pro-LBGT content being taught in schools, and expanded restrictions on books involving characters or themes related to LBGT material (along with racial justice, climate awareness, and so on) in libraries and schools. His government is seeking to shift US political life substantially to the right and entrench far-right ideologies for generations to come.

Drawing on his roots in reality television, Trump has given us a glimpse into the future of twenty-first century fascism, where brutal repression is packaged as entertaining spectacle. The arrest and indefinite detention of around a dozen pro-Palestinian student advocates was an early warning sign, sending a message to activists the country over that the new regime wouldn't be pulling any punches, to insufficiently repressive liberal university managements that they were on notice, and to supporters of Israel that the new government had their back. His deliberately staged and televised deportation of so-called Venezuelan gang members was similarly designed to strike terror into the hearts of undocumented migrants, while also casting red meat to the Republican base. So too the subsequent clash with the supposedly liberal court system, a far-right administration declaring its bona fides as a counter-revolutionary agent of change.

It is important to recognise that Trump and the broader US state are not yet capable – materially or politically – of replicating these stunts on a mass scale. But this is no argument for complacency. These terrifying incidents remain potent means of inspiring supporters and terrorising minorities and dissidents. And in the long run, they risk normalising a new authoritarianism that further erodes the very limited democratic norms that exist in the US and elsewhere, and puts all workers and the oppressed in greater danger. Like the changes ushered in by his rigging of the Supreme Court, the Trump administration's systematic replacement of liberals by MAGA operatives in the US state will have significant long-term implications for workers and the oppressed.

Trump's decision to occupy Los Angeles with Marines and the National Guard is perhaps a taste of what is to come. Events were still unfolding as this piece was written, but it's clear that Trump deliberately sought to polarise and escalate the situation as a distraction from his administration's many failures. His description of Latinos and their allies as criminals and foreign invaders combines law and order with bigoted nationalism and sets the scene for a renewed authoritarian push. The targeting of a union official, and the threats to arrest the Democratic Governor Gavin Newsome, are also highly significant. Importantly, it has been resisted.

Along with all these highly publicised measures, Trump has unleashed serious attacks on the working class. These have barely registered in the broader discussion, largely because the corporate media is more concerned about the stock market than the living standards of US workers. But this bias is reinforced by a broad left that is more likely to call the Pope a TERF[1] (?!) than notice when hundreds of millions of people are pushed further into poverty and exploitation. But nevertheless, attacks on workers are a key component of the new regime's agenda. One of its first moves was to fire one of the three remaining members of the National Labour Relations Board. This was an attempt to make all union activity null and void and was only prevented due to intervention by the court in March. Meanwhile, his draconian move to ban around two-thirds of the federal workforce from union representation stands while the courts rule on its validity, after the union's attempt at an injunction was rejected by a federal appeals court stacked with Republican judges.

Trump's war on workers extends well beyond organised labour. He has also sought to make substantial cuts to the remaining government agencies that provide desperately needed support for US workers and the poor. The mega bill currently before Congress proposes to cut around 25 percent of government spending on food stamps and kick

---

1.   Trans-Exclusionary Radical Feminist. See LGBT Rights Australia 2025.

around 8 million people off Medicaid, among other things. Trump also plans to begin cutting the (already abysmal) social security payments of those who have defaulted on their student loans by up to 15 percent as of June. All of this is necessary, it is claimed, to cover the cost of entrenching enormous tax cuts for the rich, which will cost at least $2 trillion over ten years. Overall, then, his "big beautiful bill" is set to unleash an historic attack on working-class living standards, even as it shovels more and more money into the pockets of the super-rich. An analysis by the Congressional Budget Office finds that the richest 0.1 percent will be about $390,000 a year better off as a result.

Meanwhile, in yet more proof that Trump's economic populism is purely for show, the richest man in the world was given the job of slashing "waste" in existing spending on social services. It is unclear just how much Elon Musk's Department of Government Efficiency has actually achieved, but the spectre of a billionaire and his private-school educated minions taking a chainsaw to, among other things, the departments of education and social security, sent a clear message regarding the domestic priorities of the administration. And even though Musk was eventually dumped for being a political liability, there are others in the administration with just as much zeal for "cutting red tape" as he.[2]

Imperialism unchained

Yet it is Trump's foreign policy, rather than his ruthless attacks on workers or the oppressed, that has attracted the heaviest commentary – and criticism – from the international capitalist establishment. Trump has declared war on a series of US-led institutions such as the World Health Organization, the World Trade Organization, the Paris Climate Treaty, and dramatically cut US foreign aid. He and his followers are explicit, the US is no longer prepared to be the world police. Writing for the Australian Strategic Policy Institute, Jahara Matisek and James Farwell describe the new approach:

> Gone is the era of *Pax Americana*, where the United States underwrote the global liberal order. A new framework emerges:

---

2.   Kilgore 2025.

Pact Americana. Soft power is gone, alliances are transactional, security guarantees are conditional and US strength dictates the rules of engagement.[3]

Trump's instinct is that of the mob boss, demanding an immediate payoff from every interaction. This has manifested in calls for allies to stump up more funding for organisations such as NATO and in ambitious claims during bilateral negotiations.

Nothing shows the imperial arrogance of the new administration – but also its limits – more clearly than Trump's ever-evolving tariff policy. His first targets were China, Canada and Mexico, a mix of two of the country's closest allies and its biggest rival. (To this day US tariffs on Mexico and Canada, countries that are absolutely vital to North American supply chains, remain higher than those on Russia, Cuba and North Korea.) Then came "liberation day", which saw enormous tariffs raised on a number of countries, again including long-term allies, which were taken off just a few weeks later due to turmoil in the deeper currents of the bond market and lobbying by key representatives of capital, including Musk, JP Morgan's Jamie Dimon and many others. He might be further stymied by a New York trade court's ruling that his tariffs were an illegal use of executive power, but time will tell where the Supreme Court falls on that issue.

Some, not least the administration's own spokespeople, have attempted to justify these moves as a step towards the reshoring of key manufacturing to the US. And clearly this is a goal that drives parts of the administration. Yet any serious strategy for such a drastic reorientation of world trade would have to consider Mexico and Canada as functionally parts of the US. The USA's excessive reliance on the ship-building and technological production facilities of Taiwan, Japan and South Korea is clearly a strategic weakness, yet could only be overcome gradually and with careful planning. It's hard to see how Trump's erratic policies could inspire companies to commit long-term investments worth hundreds of billions that they were not already considering. For now, US growth has slowed sharply under Trump's

---

3.   Matisek and Farwell 2025.

watch, and most of his most radical tariffs have been abandoned. Who knows what tomorrow may bring.

On the military and geopolitical front, Trump suggests both continuity and change. The Biden years saw the US involve itself in two enormous military operations – Israel's destruction of Gaza and the Ukrainian resistance to Russian occupation. In Gaza, Trump has essentially maintained the Democratic administration's policy of largely uncritical support for the Israelis. He has managed to go even further, advocating for the Strip's reinvention as a tourist destination – sans those pesky Palestinians, of course. It is hard to find words to express the horrors unfolding since Netanyahu restarted his forever war on the men, women and children of Gaza. The misery extends beyond the scope of human imagination, epitomised by pictures of emaciated children begging for assistance and body parts flying onto roofs. The barbarism unleashed on Gaza, including the deliberate targeting of hospitals and medical staff, the use of aid as a bargaining chip and so on, will likely set a new baseline for the wars to come. While governments offer only half-hearted criticism in the face of this deathscape, the global movement for Palestinian liberation continues to find ways to mobilise its supporters despite the fear of repression. It is vital that we do so, both in solidarity but also because it's very possible that Gaza could be a premonition of our collective future.

In Ukraine though, Trump, at least initially, broke more substantially with Biden's approach. Having judged that the occupied nation is not likely to return sufficient benefit on the investment of nearly $130 billion in US aid, Trump is attempting to cut his losses by forcing Ukraine to surrender. He has threatened on multiple occasions to withhold military aid and has successfully negotiated an agreement with Zelensky that will allow the US to profit from Ukraine's mineral resources. So harsh were US terms early in the negotiations that one commentator compared an earlier draft of the deal to the colonial treaties imposed on China by the European powers in the nineteenth century.[4] While the final document removes some of the most blatant neocolonial provisions, the overall message is clear and will be received

---

4.   Evans-Pritchard 2025.

by US allies the world over: protection doesn't come for free. Having said all that, there is an attempt by the US Congress, the EU and other more traditional advocates for the US empire to pull Trump back towards confrontation with Putin. As with so much else about the administration, it's unclear where things will end up. Trump's decision to end the pause on military aid to Ukraine in July and threaten Putin with tariffs if he doesn't sue for peace is only the latest twist in this geopolitical drama. Yet it's important to understand that both the pro-war and the pro-Putin wings of the US and EU establishment are entirely reactionary and should be opposed by all those on the left.

For all their specificities, Trump's policies on Gaza, Ukraine and tariffs all reflect a broader shift towards a more dangerous and aggressive imperialist posture. The bombing of Iran by the US in June is just the latest sign of this dangerous shift. The combination of resurgent nationalism, economic protectionism and increasing inter-imperialist tensions is reminiscent of periods leading up to intense global conflict and war. Some of this continues on from the work of Biden's last administration, which expanded tariffs on China and worked hard to boost US industry. But Trump has radically expanded and transformed the means of achieving these goals, seeking to bolster the profitability and competitive advantage of US enterprises – and the state as a whole – by increasing the exploitation of workers at home and by extracting surplus value from both allies and rivals abroad. To achieve this it hopes to leverage its status as the world's largest consumer market and its most powerful military machines. His preparedness to work with the Gulf states even more closely than Biden, even to the point of snubbing Netanyahu in his dealings with both Syria and Iran, is further proof of this transactional approach.

We cannot know whether the US can succeed in preventing the rise of an economically more dynamic China, and there is no political benefit to be had in guessing. What is certain is that the world working class is in an era of escalating tensions, involving both cold and hot wars, with unprecedented weapons of mass destruction at the disposal of the contending powers. There are counter-tendencies, including the interpenetration of capital and trade, and the fact that decades of inter-imperial peace means it will take time for both sides to prepare for total war. But the trajectory is terrifyingly clear. With the fraying of old US-led institutions that ran the world for much of the last century, we're also likely to see increasing violence on the margins of the world system, as with Gaza and Ukraine. Contra the campist left, Putin and Netanyahu's successes in conquering their relatively defenceless neighbours make further wars of aggression more, not less, likely.

Resistance grows

While it seemed at first that Trump's second term would be more damaging and coherent than the first, even spurring talk of fascism, Trump still has many weaknesses. To begin with, his attempt to combine far-right personalities with the more traditional Republican hard right means there are constant tensions in his administration. These tensions have been on display in the debates over visas for skilled migrants, the toing-and-froing on tariffs, Trump's decision to reverse the pause on military aid to Ukraine and the bombing of Iran. For now, the more orthodox ultra-conservatives, with their ties to big capital, have tended to win out over the more ideological extremists. Trump has then tried to compensate by ramping up far-right culture wars, hence his recent adoption of the white supremacist talking point against "white genocide" in South Africa.

Secondly, Trump remains quite unpopular. His first term saw him become the most hated president in US history, and he has already returned to similar figures just a few months into his second. This can seem at odds with the fact he won all seven swing states last November, but his victory was not a particularly decisive one. Most of the nation remained relatively unmoved by the relentless partisan debates (of incredibly little substance) that characterise US politics, with only very small changes in a handful of places delivering Trump his victory. In the end he failed to win a majority of voters, and, crucially, contin-ued the Republican tradition of losing nearly every major city to the Democratic Party. So his substantial electoral college victory reflects the fundamentally undemocratic structure of the US system, where working-class voters in big cities are under-represented in favour of relatively unpopulated rural states. To this it must be added that many workers, especially those from oppressed minorities, do not vote. This can be due to the endless logistical barriers placed in their way, but also their lack of political support for the candidates on offer. Overall then, the fact that Trump only won the support of 29 percent of US adults means that, like last time, he would be vulnerable to mass resistance.

It was hard to keep all this in perspective in the immediate aftermath of Trump's victory, which led to understandable shock on the US left, broadly defined. There was of course opposition to his attacks from the very outset, and a number of small but important local actions took place in solidarity with trans and migrant communities, among others. As well, it is significant that Republicans were advised to stop hosting traditional "town hall" public meetings to avoid public hostility[5] to the administration's reactionary policies. But at a national scale, there was a sense of paralysis, disbelief that Trump could possibly win a second time. This was reinforced by Democratic Party, which decided early on that the best thing to do was "roll over and play dead"[6] while Trump trashed working-class lives and stoked bigotry.

It seems clear that the initial period of demoralisation among those in the US opposed to Trump has come to an end. In recent months there has been a steady growth in the size and scale of street mobilisations as progressives regained confidence that they could begin to resist Trump's attacks.

Tesla dealerships were an early focal point, as activists sought to highlight Elon Musk's role in slashing essential services under the slogan "Tesla takedown". The contradiction of a company whose clients were mainly environmentally friendly progressives being operated by a sieg-heiling fascist was doomed to unravel, leading to a satisfying collapse in the company's sales and share price, as well as Musk's personal fortune. There were also small but important actions against ICE raids, and the kidnapping of pro-Palestinian student activists. However it was the nationwide "Hands Off" protests on April 5 – fortuitously timed just days after Trump's liberation day madness – that created a new feeling of confidence. The day saw strong turnouts across all fifty states, including all sorts of small country towns as well as major urban centres. This was quickly followed by sizeable, if not

5.   Jimison 2025.
6.   Carville 2025.

overwhelming, demonstrations on 19 April and 1 May, and then even larger "No Kings" rallies on 14 June. Along with Musk's sidelining and Trump's tariff backflips, these rallies have given confidence to the resistance and will encourage further action. Opposition to Trump's anti-migrant agenda has also taken the form of increasingly militant actions against ICE raids. The dramatic protests in LA in June were only the tip of the iceberg, with local actions against ICE occurring across the country. The bravery of often small numbers of people to intervene and try to stop arrests and deportations is particularly encouraging.

The popular opposition to Trump has encouraged greater institutional pushback against the worst excesses of Trump's agenda. After Columbia's early cowardice, a number of universities, notably Harvard, have taken a stronger stand against Trump's intervention into their institutions. University managements – not to mention their staff and students – tend to be implicated in liberal networks of fundraising and organising, overwhelmingly tied to the Democratic Party. This helps to explain why Republicans despise them so, but also why their leaders have an interest in pushing back. It's likely that campuses will remain an important flashpoint for struggles over curriculum, staff cuts, democratic rights on campus, and so on. Broadly, however, corporate opposition to Trump has been extremely limited, with most preferring to stay silent and avoid a confrontation with the president. Importantly, in the rare cases it has manifested, this type of opposition has focused overwhelmingly on issues that affect corporate profits, such as tariffs, not on the attacks targeting the vast majority of Americans.

As with all political movements, the growing resistance to Trump throws up political questions that need to be worked through. What exactly is being resisted? And what is the end goal? The Democratic Party machine argues that Trump is an outlier, a freak accident in the US political system. It follows that he can and should be defeated at the next electoral opportunity, and things can go back to normal.

The truth is that the US, like all capitalist states, has a long history of anti-democratic, bigoted and far-right politics. Its history of slavery and Jim Crow remains embedded in its social structure to this day, despite the formal equality won in the 1960s. And the mainstream institutions of the capitalist class and state – here we should include the courts, the police and military forces, the intelligence services, the Democratic and Republican parties, the universities and the corporate media – have never been a bulwark against such things. Indeed they have more often been the agents of it. Thus Barack Obama remains the president responsible for the most deportations in US history, the liberal *New York Times* supported the slaughter in Iraq, Afghanistan and now Gaza, and the police, FBI and CIA have consistently sided against democracy for as long as they have existed.

These terrible facts suggest that defending the status quo prior to Trump – and the despicable institutions that maintained it – is untenable for anyone seeking justice, either for US workers or for the many victims of US imperialism. Yet this is precisely what many of the mainstream organisers and media spokespeople for the resistance would have people do. Their goal is to keep the protests that take place as set-piece actions of reactive opposition to Trump's excesses, rather than allow them to develop a progressive vision for the transformation of US society. This also explains why Palestine is so often left off the agenda, as Democrats share Trump's undying support for Israel. And as midterms and the 2028 presidential election edge closer, the pressure will be to fall in behind every corporate Democrat regardless of their stance on key questions. In these conditions, the task of the left is to find creative ways of engaging with the broader resistance all the while fighting to win a minority to a more radical perspective.

Global reverberations

It might have been expected that Trump's victory would prompt a surge in the fortunes of the international far right. Capturing the US state is by far their biggest win globally, and would seem to reinforce the likes of Modi, Meloni, Orbán and others. And clearly he has shifted the Overton window dramatically to the right in a series of ways, and the far right continues to make gains, as seen recently in Portugal and Spain. The contradiction, however, is that Trump's America First approach has led to a nationalist backlash in country after country, placing some local fascists in an uncomfortable position. There have been three broad approaches to this problem. Some, like Marine Le Pen in France, have denounced Trump's approach to international relations and declared their intention to defend their country against him. This has the benefit of appealing to the political mainstream, but risks alienating the more ideological of their supporters. Elsewhere, figures like Italy's Giorgia Meloni have tried to act as mediators, emphasising their shared reactionary values in order to leverage better trade outcomes, while maintaining some independence. Then there are figures such as Modi who have revelled in finding themselves so ideologically in sync with an American administration. They risk being accused of prostrating their nation at the feet of a foreign leader, a reactionary line of argument that has been deployed effectively by centrists in places as diverse as Canada and India. These dynamics are unstable and will continue to shift as Trump's policies evolve.

But while the far right remains somewhat awkwardly positioned, the political centre has been quite effective in using Trump as a means of cohering and galvanising themselves. In Canada, Romania and Australia, establishment forces have been able to channel widespread hostility to Trump to dramatically shift electoral outcomes. In France and Germany, centre-right parties have attempted to use Trump's erratic imperial policy to justify massive rearmament drives and a more aggressive foreign posture. There is now talk of the need to broaden Europe's nuclear defence policy, a terrifying prospect given the tensions in Ukraine and elsewhere. In France also, it's possible that ruling-class fury with Trump bolstered the High Court's confidence to ban Le Pen from the 2027 presidential election.

None of this has meant the centre is breaking with the reactionary social and economic values the far right espouses. Indeed, the opposite is true, as policies and ideas that were once seen as fringe continue to be normalised. Britain's Keir Starmer is a perfect example of this dynamic, with his persistent and highly inflammatory attacks on migrants and refugees, support for the dramatic curtailing of trans and women's rights by the High Court, and cuts to essential services and payments relied on by millions of workers. In this context, every political defeat of the far right feels temporary, their return almost inevitable. To break out of this cycle it is essential that the revolutionary left continues to grow and build its capacity to provide an alternative political pole and a way out of the social, economic and climate crises facing our world.

Australia: a global outlier

For decades Australia has been something of an outlier. Economically, it enjoyed a long boom between the 1990s and 2013, and saw living standards rising consistently, if anaemically. Politically the country has been remarkably stable: while the rest of the world deals with the rise of new parties, or the transformation of existing ones into something unrecognisable, our two-party system remains largely intact. There are counter-tendencies, including the phenomenon of party leaders lasting less than a term and the rise in the percentage of voters supporting candidates outside the big four parties. But compared with similar nations the situation has remained remarkably stable, as Australia's success in cashing in on China's rise allowed it to ride out the global financial crisis and even the COVID pandemic with relative ease.

Further reinforcing this stability, Australia has not seen any sort of mass far-right force emerge either within or outside the parliamentary framework. This is partly explained by the country's recent social and economic history, but not completely. There clearly is a hard-right minority who could be radicalised and organised by a capable and interventionist political current, and the votes of the various fragments tallied around 13.6 percent nationally in the Senate in the most recent election. But the Australian far right does not impact politics anywhere near as much as its support would suggest. In part this is because its main leader, Pauline Hanson, is incompetent, ageing, rurally-based, and does not appeal to young voters. Conversely, its most dynamic extra-parliamentary grouping, the National Socialist Network, is tiny and espouses Nazism, which makes it impossible to connect with a sizeable audience. Along with the billionaire Clive Palmer's amateurish interventions, it's been difficult for a new right to emerge that is more solidly organised and rooted in the cities. So for now, though its vote is stable, the far right remains fragmented and ineffectual.

There was potential for all this to change with the post-COVID surge in inflation, which saw a sharp drop in the living standards of Australian workers for the first time in a generation. Taking into account the cost of elevated mortgage repayments, the Australia Institute estimated that real wages in 2024 had declined by an average of $8,000 – or 12.4 percent – since 2021.[7] This was due to inflation, of course, but also the pathetic inaction of the union officials. These so-called leaders allowed their members' wages to go backwards at a rate of knots, all the while cynically celebrating the achievements (sic) of the Labor government. Their failure is made even clearer given the historically low rates of unemployment, a situation which gives workers enormous bargaining power. In these conditions, it seemed as if a relatively conservative Labor government was set to be punished, as with so many other incumbents. Polls late in 2024 showed Labor set for minority government at best, and even left open the possibility of an historic return to opposition after just one term.

Yet just a few months later, Labor is ascendant following a smashing victory over the Liberal and National parties in the 2025 federal election. How to explain this stunning turnaround? Many mainstream pundits blame Dutton's terrible campaign, in which it seemed every week a new policy or talking point was rolled out and then abandoned after coming under political fire. But his support was dropping well before the campaign officially began. And it's doubtful whether many people pay much attention to the chattering classes and their inane daily commentary on the campaign trail. Others have suggested that the influence of the right-wing Murdoch media empire is falling to an all-time low. This is partly because the Murdoch press has drifted so far to the right as to make it nearly unreadable for anyone to the left of Genghis Khan.

A more compelling argument given for the result is that it is a refutation of Trumpism and the attempts by the Liberal Party to import it into Australia. There is clearly some truth to this, with a range of polls showing that the majority despise the US president. While this is definitely a positive sign, one caveat is that it is not clear how much of this hostility relates to his reactionary social agenda, as opposed to his generally chaotic approach to governance. Certainly Labor did not run strongly on issues such as Indigenous or LGBT rights, let alone climate change. And they refused to openly attack Trump, relying instead on indirect references to "politics imported from elsewhere". But they

---

7.   Richardson and Jericho 2024.

were able to slam Peter Dutton for his flirtation with Trump's policies – including attacks on working from home, public servants, putting the far-right Jacinta Price in charge of a local DOGE. And Labor benefited from the fact that inflation had stabilised, and real wages were no longer falling.

Dutton's Trump-lite policies were widely seen as prefiguring an assault on workers' wages and conditions – particularly those of white-collar women – and the essential social services, like Medicare, that make life bearable. These are the precise themes that Labor based their campaign on. This is an important point that can be obscured by simplistic comparisons with the Canadian election, where a former central banker gained heavily by posing himself as an opponent of Trump in aggressively nationalist terms. In Australia Labor did not run a right-wing nationalist campaign. If anything, they drew more deeply on social democratic motifs – albeit in typically tepid fashion – than at any time during their term. Their policy announcements focused on providing more support to workers by cutting student debt by 20 percent, increasing funding to Medicare, increasing childcare funding, and providing a (minuscule) progressive income tax break. Another difference was that in Canada the Liberal vote grew by cannibalising the rest of the progressive vote. In Australia, the election represented a clear, though modest, shift to the left, a result that wildly bucks the international trend. Traditional swing voters chose Labor or independents over the Liberals, all except the wealthiest Greens voters stuck with the party – and it picked up more working-class votes than ever – despite its relatively progressive positioning, and serious socialist candidates won good results across Melbourne.

The corporate media, of course, have no interest in such an interpretation, and instead chose to highlight the marginal swings that resulted in three out of four Greens MPs losing their seats as evidence of a rejection of extremism "on both sides". According to them, the Greens were battered for their "radical" stance against Israel's genocide in Gaza, and for their "disruption" of Labor's pro-developer housing policies. This narrative is being used by people inside and outside the party to argue for a shift back to the centre. This was prefigured in the final months before the election, when the Greens adjusted their messaging to being primarily about attacking Dutton as the main enemy, encouraging the idea that blocking the Liberals was the key issue in this election. The appointment of Larissa Waters as new leader would suggest a compromise between the left and right wings of the party is on the cards, but time will tell.

In this context, the national expansion of Victorian Socialists is an important step to consolidate the gains won in Melbourne, and can help both to put pressure on the Greens to maintain their leftish stances, while also giving left-wing and disenfranchised working-class voters a vitally needed anti-capitalist alternative. The construction of this kind of united socialist front in the electoral arena is of course just one part of building a stronger revolutionary movement in Australia, but it has already shown its capacity to popularise socialist politics in working-class communities, strengthen existing extra-parliamentary organising, and generate space for new campaigns moving forward.

Overall then, it is very positive that the right, led by Dutton and other extremists in the Coalition, failed to lead more than a small minority behind a Trump-like agenda. As a result, unlike in nearly every comparable country, the far-right bogey cannot be deployed to justify a shift to the right on social issues. The strong Labor majority means there are no excuses now for inaction on the various issues of importance to the left and working-class people. Housing affordability remains a permanent crisis for working-class people that the corporate obsession with increasing supply will do little to fix. Workers who have suffered years of declining wages, such as teachers, health professionals and others, could feel more confident to take action now that the economy has stabilised. Trump remains a lightning rod for opposition, a permanent factor of instability and resistance. The Albanese government's support for the US's bombing of Iran, the AUKUS submarine deal and Jillian Segal's fake "antisemitism" plan have already made the priorities of the Labor Party clear.

But through all of this, Gaza. An unspeakable, unfathomable crime. A concentration camp and a holocaust, broadcast live. A daily reminder that resistance is essential but insufficient, that we urgently need to overthrow an international capitalist class capable of enabling these unthinkable horrors. If not now, when?

References

Carville, James 2025, "It's Time for a Daring Political Maneuver, Democrats", *New York Times*, 25 February. https://www.nytimes.com/2025/02/25/opinion/democrats-trump-congress.html

Evans-Pritchard, Ambrose 2025, "'Never seen anything like it': Trump's outrageous new Ukraine deal", *Financial Review*, 28 March. https://www.afr.com/world/europe/us-seeks-far-reaching-control-over-investment-in-ukraine-20250328-p5ln63

Jimison, Robert 2025, "Republicans Face Angry Voters at Town Halls, Hinting at Broader Backlash", *New York Times*, 23 February. https://www.nytimes.com/2025/02/23/us/politics/republicans-congress-town-halls-trump.html

Kilgore, Ed 2025, "DOGE May Not Need Elon Musk Anymore", *Intelligencer*, https://nymag.com/intelligencer/article/doge-may-not-need-elon-musk-anymore.html

LGBT Rights Australia 2025, "TERF POPE", 9 May. https://www.facebook.com/EMRAUST/posts/pfbid0296jCeyBna2bxGZsGZkB1FqQMHQHRaNNNLSG1CQUk-fxNt7B73wK9xN3g54B4Xq1Mml

Matisek, Jahara and James Farwell 2025, "Trump's national security strategy: from *Pax Americana* to Pact Americana", *The Strategist*, Australian Strategic Policy Institute, 2 May. https://www.aspistrategist.org.au/trumps-national-security-strategy-from-pax-americana-to-pact-americana/

Richardson, David and Greg Jericho 2024, "Wages are growing faster than inflation – but workers are $8,000 worse off than 3 years ago", *The Australia Institute*, 13 November. https://australiainstitute.org.au/post/wages-are-growing-faster-than-inflation-but-workers-are-8000-worse-off-than-3-years-ago/

MICK ARMSTRONG

Marxism and National Liberation

Mick Armstrong is the co-author of *The Labor Party: a Marxist Analysis* and *The Fight for Workers' Power: Revolution and Counter-Revolution in the 20th Century*, and has written widely on revolutionary organisation and the Australian labour movement.

THE WAR ON Palestine and Lebanon has sharply posed a series of theoretical and strategic questions for Marxists. What is the relationship between the struggle for national independence and the broader struggle for human liberation? What social forces have the potential to defeat Israeli colonial settler rule and its imperialist backers? Does an alliance of the working class of Palestine and the broader Arab world with bourgeois and petty-bourgeois nationalist forces, such as Hamas and Hezbollah, offer a way forward? What are the tasks of socialists in the imperialist heartlands? Should socialists adhere to a two-stage approach of limiting the struggle to a first stage of winning an independent capitalist nation state and then a later second stage of a struggle for socialism? Or alternatively should Marxists break with a stages approach and attempt to carry the struggle for national liberation over into a struggle for workers' power?

Marxists standing in the tradition of Lenin and Trotsky have long supported the right of national self-determination, including the right of an oppressed nation to secede from the state that dominates it.[1] As Lenin put it in 1916: "This is an absolute demand, even where the chance of secession being possible and 'practicable' before the introduction of socialism is only one in a thousand".[2] Consequently the Bolsheviks backed the right of the oppressed nations of the tsarist Empire – Poland, Ukraine, Finland, Latvia and various others – to break away from Russian rule and establish their own nation-state. The Bolsheviks also supported the right of the oppressed populations of the colonial world to revolt against imperialist rule. These were basic democratic rights that socialists needed to champion, while fighting to take them further to challenge the whole capitalist order. As Lenin wrote in *The right of nations to self-determination*, his polemic against Rosa Luxemburg and her supporters, who opposed the demand for national self-determination:

> The bourgeois nationalism of *any* oppressed nation has a general democratic content that is directed *against* oppression, and it is this content that we *unconditionally* support. At the same time we strictly distinguish it from the tendency towards national exclusiveness; we fight against the tendency of the Polish bourgeois to oppress the Jews, etc., etc.[3]

Supporting national self-determination for oppressed nations was also seen by Marxists as important to combatting reactionary nationalist prejudices among workers of oppressor nations. As Marx noted in his writings on Ireland, workers in an oppressor nation like Britain would be incapable of achieving their own liberation if they backed their rulers oppressing another nation. In 1869 he wrote:

> [I]t is in the direct and absolute interests of the English working class to get rid of their present connexion with Ireland ... The English working class will never accomplish anything before

1.   See for example Lenin 1914 and Trotsky 1997, pp.889–913.
2.   Lenin 1916, p.346.
3.   Lenin 1914, p.412.

> it has got rid of Ireland ... This is why the Irish question is so
> important for the social movement in general.[4]

As well, Lenin and the Bolsheviks argued that revolts in the colonies and by oppressed national minorities in Europe could *potentially* destabilise capitalist rule in the imperialist heartlands. Of course, not every struggle for national independence has provoked a major crisis for the imperialist power. British capitalism was not ruptured by Kenyan, Ugandan, Cypriot or Iraqi independence, or US capitalism by Filipino independence, or Australian capitalism by Papua New Guinean independence. The world-wide radicalising impact of the American war in Vietnam was, however, a decisive confirmation of the destabilising potential of national liberation struggles. The validity of the Bolsheviks' strategic insight was further demonstrated by the 1974 Portuguese revolution, sparked by Portugal's defeat in its colonial wars in Africa.[5]

However this principled Bolshevik approach of supporting the right of national self-determination does not tell you what specific political orientation socialists in the *oppressed* nation should adopt to win their national and social freedom. What demands should they raise? How should they relate to other class forces in the national movement – in particular, should they engage in cross-class alliances and politically support bourgeois/petty-bourgeois nationalist forces?

The Second International's dubious record

In the late nineteenth century and early twentieth century the level of development of capitalist industry was still very limited in most colonial countries. The social forces had not yet matured to open up the prospect of the emerging working class winning the leadership of the national independence movement and going on to seriously challenge capitalist rule. Moreover the Second Socialist International offered little useful advice or support to the small groups of socialists that developed in the colonial world prior to World War I. The right wing of the Second International was sympathetic to colonialism. Opposition

---

4.   Marx and Engels 1989, p.398.
5.   Geier 2024.

to colonialism was only narrowly carried at the 1907 Stuttgart Congress of the International, by a vote of 127 to 108. Edward David, a leading right-wing revisionist in the German Social Democratic Party, argued that "Europe needs colonies. It does not have enough of them".[6] The left wing of the movement opposed colonialism but by and large downplayed the potential for building a socialist movement in the colonies. In the case of Ireland British socialists generally backed the bourgeois nationalists' demand for Home Rule (self-government under the British Crown).

In this context it is understandable that the groups of socialists that first emerged in the colonial countries confined their approach to the undoubtedly necessary tasks of laying the basis for a working-class movement, helping to form trade unions and campaigning for greater democratic rights. When it came to the national question, reflecting the orientation of the Socialist International, they in many cases confined their demands to supporting the establishment of an independent *bourgeois* republic. That is the same demand as the various petty-bourgeois and bourgeois nationalists. But with economic development and the further growth of the working class in the colonies, in semi-colonies like Iran, Turkey and China and in the oppressed nations of the Russian Empire, the approach of socialists limiting themselves to supporting bourgeois nationalists and independent capitalist republics posed serious problems. It led to needless defeats for the emerging working-class movement.

By the early twentieth century it was clear that the wealthy classes in colonies like India and Egypt – the landlords, the merchants, the industrial capitalists and so on – were hesitant about challenging the colonial powers. They might like the idea of national independence and the expansion of the market for local industry. However to achieve independence meant mobilising the exploited mass of the population – the peasantry, the urban poor and the working class – to confront imperial power. That was a risky operation – an operation that could well threaten their wealth and power. So they prevaricated. When mass revolts broke out in countries like China they commonly went beyond

---

6.   Riddell 1984, pp.6, 15.

the narrow limits of demands for national independence. Peasants seized the land from landlords. Workers struck, not just against imperialist-owned companies, but against the local bourgeoisie. This in turn posed the question: why should workers and the oppressed give their lives fighting to drive out the colonial power but then limit themselves to installing a capitalist government, under which they would continue to be exploited and oppressed, if this time by local capitalists?

Possibly the first group of socialists in a colonial country to seriously grapple with this question was the small Irish Socialist Republican Party (ISRP) founded by James Connolly in 1896. Ireland, though still a predominantly agricultural society, was more economically advanced than most British colonies. Moreover it had a long history of revolts against English rule, in the course of which, as Irish Republican leader Wolfe Tone noted as early as the 1790s, the "men of property" – the petty capitalists, the landlords and other exploiting layers – when push came to shove temporised or backed England against the "men of no property". From this bitter experience the ISRP declared in their 1896 program that British rule served "the interests of the exploiting classes of both nations" and consequently "the national and economic freedom of the Irish people must be sought" by "the establishment of an Irish Socialist Republic, and the consequent conversion of the means of production, distribution and exchange into the common property of society, to be held and controlled by a democratic state in the interests of the entire community".[7] More than just fighting British rule, workers had to raise their own class demands and challenge Irish bosses and landlords. The ISRP opposed limiting the national struggle to the demand for Home Rule advocated by mainstream bourgeois nationalists and counterposed the demand for a workers' republic to the traditional demand of a capitalist republic championed by the Republican wing of the nationalists, who advocated armed struggle against British rule.

However the ISRP's stance was an exception. Prior to the 1917 Russian revolution most parties in the Socialist International did not seriously address the question of what strategy colonial socialists

---

7.   Lynch 2005, p.40.

should adopt in relation to bourgeois nationalists. Most Western social-ists held to the view that the less advanced economies would essentially follow the trajectory of development traced previously by the industri-ally advanced capitalist states. According to this view the workers in the colonies would simply have to wait for their day to arrive. There were some partial exceptions to this pattern. In 1898 the First Congress of the Russian Social Democratic Labour Party (RSDLP) declared: "The further east one goes in Europe, the more the bourgeoisie becomes in the political respect weaker, more cowardly, and meaner, and the larger are the cultural and political tasks which fall to the share of the proletariat".[8] Leon Trotsky took this approach further with his theory of permanent revolution, elaborated in his book *Results and Prospects* in the context of the 1905 Russian revolution.[9] But at that stage Trotsky did not generalise permanent revolution to the colonial world. As for Lenin, he rather naively argued in 1912:

> What has decayed is the Western bourgeoisie, which is already confronted by its grave digger, the proletariat. But in Asia there is *still* a bourgeoisie capable of championing sincere, militant, consistent democracy, a worthy comrade of France's great men of the Enlightenment and great leaders of the close of the eighteenth century.[10]

The impact of the Russian revolution

In the course of the 1917 revolution the Bolsheviks had to come to grips with the concrete questions posed as the tsarist empire was torn apart by social and national struggle. It was not sufficient for Marxists to just say they supported the right of national self-determination in Ukraine, Poland, Finland and the like. What about the class struggle in these oppressed nations? The issue was brought to a head in Ukraine, then an overwhelmingly peasant country much more economically backward than the Middle East today. In the aftermath of the February Revolution

---

8.   Quoted in Hallas 2003, p.25.
9.   Trotsky 1969.
10. Lenin 1912, p.165.

a petty-bourgeois nationalist government, the Rada, rose to power in Ukraine and began to demand independence. The Provisional government in Petrograd, backed by the Menshevik reformists, denounced any idea of Ukrainian independence. Only the Bolsheviks supported the rights of the Ukrainians.

That did not, however, lead the Bolsheviks to *politically* support the Rada. The Rada was neither a friend of the Ukrainian workers nor an opponent of imperialism. The Rada supported the German invasion of Ukraine and later carried out pogroms against Ukraine's Jewish population. In opposition to the Rada the Bolsheviks and their working-class supporters backed the formation of a Ukrainian soviet government.[11] This became the Bolsheviks' approach in other oppressed nations of the tsarist Empire. They were for working-class rule with the support of the peasantry, not bourgeois republics. Summing up this experience Trotsky wrote in his *History of the Russian Revolution*:

> [I]n the course of her three revolutions, you can find every variant of national and class struggle except one: that in which the bourgeoisie of any oppressed nation played a liberating role in relation to its own people. At every stage of its development every borderland bourgeoisie, no matter in what colours it might dance, was invariably dependent upon the central banks, trusts, and commercial institutions which were in essence the agents of all Russian capital... Taken as a whole, the bourgeoisie of the oppressed nation played the same role in relation to the ruling bourgeoisie that the latter played in relation to international finance capital. The complex hierarchy of antagonisms and dependencies did not remove for one single day the fundamental solidarity of the three in the struggle against the insurrectionary masses.
>
> In the sum total the bourgeoisie of the oppressed nations manifested no less hostility to the revolution than the Great Russian bourgeoisie.[12]

---

11.   See Armstrong 2016.
12.   Trotsky 1997, pp.909–10.

The Bolsheviks, the early Comintern and the colonial revolution

In the first years after the Russian revolution the Bolsheviks' views on the national question were in flux. Initially influential sections of the party generalised the approach adopted in the October Revolution to the colonies, effectively embracing Trotsky's theory of permanent revolution. In this period Trotsky's *Results and Prospects* was reprinted several times, including foreign language editions.[13] This was the orientation Nikolai Bukharin (previously an opponent of national self-determination) and Evgenii Preobrazhensky advocated in their 1920 book, *The ABC of Communism, which was* for a period *the* textbook of Bolshevik politics. *The ABC of Communism* provided an elaboration of the recently revised party program. It emphasised that the new program explicitly abandoned the old 1903 RSDLP program that had not envisaged workers taking power. The new program called for "the establishment of working class rule" and called for world socialist revolution. Bukharin and Preobrazhensky wrote:

> The demand for a soviet regime has in fact become the international watchword of the proletariat. In [my emphasis] countries the workers sound this war-cry, in conjunction with the demand for the dictatorship of the proletariat. Life has confirmed the accuracy of our slogan, "All power to the soviets", not in Russia alone, but in *every* [my emphasis] country where there is a proletariat.[14]

At the First Congress of the Communist International (Comintern) in March 1919, which, however, had a limited attendance, there was no detailed discussion of the national question. The Congress Manifesto did denounce "colonial slavery" and hail the revolts in the colonies. It pointed out:

> The liberation of the colonies is possible only together with the liberation of the working class in the imperialist centres. The

---

13. Pantsov 2000, p.15.
14. Bukharin and Preobrazhensky 1920.

workers and peasants, not only of Annam, Algeria, and Bengal, but also of Persia and Armenia, will gain the possibility of an independent existence only when the workers of Britain and France have toppled Lloyd George and Clemenceau and taken state power into their own hands.

Colonial slaves of Africa and Asia: the hour of proletarian dictatorship in Europe will also be the hour of your liberation![15]

Significantly it argued: "Already today, the struggle in the more developed colonies is waged not merely under the banner of national liberation but immediately acquires a clearly defined social character".[16]

However by the time of the Second Comintern Congress in July/August 1920 there had been a shift in the approach of some leading Bolsheviks. There was greater emphasis on fighting British imperialism, which was seen as the main threat to the survival of the Russian revolution, and a subsequent search for allies to oppose the British. The Second Congress held a substantial discussion of the national and colonial question. The Congress debates were a major step forward and contained a number of vital insights. However there were also certain confusions, and some important strategic issues were not fully addressed. This in part reflected the uneven level of economic and political development in the colonial and semi-colonial world and the as yet very limited experience of Communist activity in these countries. The theses adopted correctly noted that it was not necessary for colonies to go through a capitalist stage of development; that with assistance of workers' revolutions in the advanced capitalist countries it would be possible for colonies to skip the capitalist stage and begin to build genuine socialist societies. The Theses on the Colonial Question argued:

A resolute struggle must be waged against the attempt to clothe the revolutionary liberation movements in the backward countries which are not genuinely communist in communist

---

15.   Riddell 1987, pp.227–28.
16.   Riddell 1987, p.227.

colours. The Communist International has the duty of supporting the revolutionary movement in the colonies and backward countries only with the object of rallying the constituent elements of the future proletarian parties – which will be truly communist and not only in name – in all the backward countries and educating them to a consciousness of their special task, namely, that of fighting against the bourgeois-democratic trend in their nation. The Communist International should collaborate provisionally with the revolutionary movement of the colonies and backward countries, and even form an alliance with it, but it must not amalgamate with it; it must unconditionally maintain the independence of the proletarian movement, even if it is only in an embryonic stage.[17]

The Commission on the Colonial Question amended Lenin's draft thesis, which called for communists to support "bourgeois national" movements against imperialism. It was pointed out that many bourgeois nationalist forces collaborated with imperialism and were in no sense genuinely revolutionary. Instead the formula "national-revolutionary" was substituted for "bourgeois national". This was a fudge that did not clarify the issue. Other than the exploited masses of the working class and peasantry, who undoubtedly were genuinely revolutionary, what other social class, if any, was to be included under the rubric "national-revolutionary"? In the imperialist era the reality was that none of the bourgeois forces in the colonial world, as was decisively demonstrated during the 1925–27 Chinese revolution, were consistently revolutionary. All of them flip-flopped around from a "revolutionary" position of support for armed struggle to end colonial rule to cutting a deal with the imperialist powers.

In his address to the Congress Lenin tried to get around this problem by arguing "that as communists we will only support the bourgeois freedom movements...if these movements are really revolutionary and if their representatives are not opposed to us training and organising

---

17.   Degras 1971, pp.143–44.

the peasantry in a revolutionary way".[18] But which bourgeois figure with even half a brain was going to allow the Communists to do that?

In a few colonies a working-class movement had emerged. What was to be the approach there? The Indian socialist MN Roy argued at the Second Congress and in subsequent Comintern debates that in colonies like India the working class in alliance with the peasantry was the force that needed to lead the struggle against British rule and establish a soviet republic. Lenin had some sympathy for Roy's views. However despite Roy's supplementary theses being unanimously adopted they were subsequently ignored.

No clear guidelines were given at the Second Congress on a key strategic question that was soon to confront Communists in countries like China. When should revolutionaries and the working-class movement break decisively with the nationalists and rally the peasantry, the urban poor and other intermediary layers behind them and carry the struggle for independence over into a struggle for workers' power? Given the limited experience of the colonial Communist parties, that question could not yet be fully settled. But it was a decisive question that the new Communist parties were to be confronted with head on. Getting it wrong had disastrous consequences.

There was no substantial discussion of the colonial question at the Third Comintern Congress in June 1921. However Trotsky, in his report "On the World Economic Crisis and the New Tasks of the Communist International", insisted that a colonial bourgeoisie's

> struggle against foreign imperialist domination cannot...be either consistent or energetic in as much as the native bourgeoisie itself is intimately bound up with foreign capital... Only the rise of a native proletariat strong enough numerically and capable of struggle can provide a real axis for the revolution. In comparison to the country's entire population, the size of the Indian proletariat is, of course, numerically small, but those who have grasped the meaning of the revolution's development in Russian will never fail to take into account that the proletariat's

---

18. Second Congress of the Communist International, p.111.

revolutionary role in the Oriental countries will far exceed its actual numerical strength.[19]

The Fourth Comintern Congress of November/December 1922 saw a further major discussion of the colonial question. The theses adopted re-emphasised a number of points, including the key role of the anti-colonial struggle and the importance of Communist parties in the imperialist powers backing revolts in the colonies, combatting racist prejudices and providing solidarity and support to the emerging colonial Communist parties. It also highlighted the fact that "native ruling classes tend to make compromises with foreign capitalism that are directed against the interests of the popular masses".[20] The theses declared:

> [T]he Communist International supports every national-revolutionary movement against imperialism. However, it does not ignore the fact that the oppressed masses can be led to victory only by a consistent revolutionary line aimed at drawing the broadest masses into active struggle and an unconditional break with all those who seek conciliation with imperialism in order to maintain their own class-rule.

They went on to stress that:

> only the agrarian revolution, which adopts the aim of expropriating large landholdings, can set the mighty peasant masses in motion… Bourgeois nationalists…fear agrarian slogans and seek every possibility to water them down. This reveals the close links of the native bourgeoisie with the feudal and feudal-bourgeois great landowners, on whom they are ideologically and politically dependent. All revolutionary forces must utilise this vacillation to reveal the irresolution of the bourgeois leaders of the nationalist movements.

---

19.   Quoted in Pantsov 2000, p.101.
20.   Riddell 2012, p.1187.

Any refusal of Communists...to take part in the struggle against imperialist tyranny, on the excuse of supposed "defence" of independent class interests, is opportunism of the worst sort that can only discredit the proletarian revolution in the East. No less damaging is the attempt to remain aloof from the struggle for the immediate interests of the working class in order to pursue "national unity" or "civil peace" with the bourgeois democrats.

The Communist workers' parties...have a double task: both to fight for the most radically possible resolution of the tasks of a bourgeois-democratic revolution, aimed at winning political independence, and also to organise the worker and peasant masses in struggle for their particular class interests, profiting from all the contradictions in the nationalist bourgeois-democratic camp.

The workers' movement...must strive above all to achieve the role of an independent revolutionary force in the overall anti-imperialist front. Only when its autonomous weight is acknowledged and its political independence is thus safeguarded is it permissible and necessary to conclude temporary agreements with bourgeois democracy. The proletariat supports immediate demands...to the degree that the current relationship of forces does not permit it to implement its soviet programme as an immediate task.[21]

Despite these fundamentally correct theses, major speeches by Karl Radek and GI Safarov highlighted the fact that leading Comintern officials still had considerable illusions in the supposed objective revolutionary potential of bourgeois nationalist forces and even of the "moribund feudal class". Radek declared:

They will try a thousand times to sell themselves to this or that faction of world capitalism; they will try a thousand times to

---

21.   Riddell 2012, pp.1182–87.

betray the revolutionary interests of their country, but the joke of history is that…they've got no choice. They must fight, because in the long run a compromise with imperialism is impossible.

…our task consists of…first, organising the young working class, and second, establishing a proper relationship between them and the *objectively* [my emphasis] revolutionary bourgeois forces.[22]

Safarov stated that a "bourgeois-democratic government in the backward countries provides support and great reassurance for our proletarian movement". Communists were to pay a heavy price for these illusions.

Radek also severely underestimated the revolutionary possibilities in China, arguing that "neither the victory of socialism nor the establishment of a soviet republic is on the agenda. Unfortunately, even the question of national unity has not yet been historically placed on the agenda in China".[23] This assessment did not help Chinese Communists prepare themselves politically for the revolution that was soon to sweep the country.

Turkey and Iran: two difficult early tests

Communists were quickly confronted with challenges when it came to applying a principled revolutionary approach to the national question. The Turkish case, in particular, was far from straightforward.[24] The Ottoman Empire, ruling over much of the Middle East and North Africa, allied with Germany in World War I. With its defeat in the war Ottoman territories were carved up by Britain and France; even the Empire's Turkish core came under threat with the British occupying Istanbul and supporting a Greek invasion of Anatolia in 1921.

There was no popular revolt against this imperialist-backed invasion. Workers were largely passive, as was the great bulk of the peasantry. The Turkish army was plagued by mass desertions. However the officer corps proved loyal to the nationalist military dictator Kemal

---

22.   Riddell 2012, pp.732–33.
23.   Riddell 2012, p.733.
24.   See Harris 1992, Carr 1966 and 1972 and Uzun 2004.

Ataturk. These Kemalist officers had presided over the Armenian genocide at the start of World War I. They followed that up with massacres of the Empire's Arab population and went on to persecute the substantial Greek minority. According to Turkish socialist Cem Uzun, "1,200,000 'Greeks' (actually Orthodox Christians, some of whom spoke Turkish) were expelled… This decapitated the working class, and weakened virtually any form of potential opposition".[25] The Kemalists were supported by the small layer of nationalist intellectuals and bureaucrats and rich Turkish Muslims, who had benefited from the looting of the property of Christians.[26]

The Greek army advanced rapidly into Anatolia. It seemed the Turkish forces were going to be decisively defeated. The tide was turned largely due to the financial and military support provided to the Kemalists by Soviet Russia and the emergence in Greece of a working class-based anti-war movement.[27] The Bolsheviks were correct to defend Turkish national rights from imperialist invasion. The Bolsheviks also rightly feared that a successful invasion would increase the likelihood of a British attack on Soviet territory. This setback for imperialism was a good thing and Britain was forced to evacuate Istanbul. However the nationalist regime the Bolsheviks armed was in no sense a revolutionary anti-imperialist government or even a liberal democratic one. It was an anti-working class dictatorship that ethnically cleansed what had been an increasingly militant working class. Turkish Communists faced mass executions. In a notorious case the Kemalists drowned CP leader Mustafa Subhi and 16 other leading communists in the Sea of Trebizond in January 1921.[28]

Having defeated the imperialist-backed invasion, the Turkish nationalists quickly began to distance themselves from their former Soviet allies, seeking a reproachment with British imperialism. In 1924 and 1925 sharpening British hostility to Turkish expansionist ambitions in Iraq pushed the Kemalists back towards the Bolsheviks, leading to the signing of a Soviet-Turkish treaty of neutrality. There

---

25.   Uzun 2004, p.187.
26.   Uzun 2004, pp.140–47.
27.   On the Marxist attitude to military support see Draper 1969.
28.   Harris 1992, p.118.

was, however, no let-up in the persecution of Communists and of trade union organisation. As Cem Uzun summed up:

> The result of the war was a defeat for imperialism, but it was far from a victory for the Turkish people. Ethnic cleansing had torn the heart out of society. It had also help smash the working-class movement. The forces in Turkish society capable of fighting from below for democracy and social change had been dramatically weakened.[29]

Among the Bolsheviks, desperate for allies in the face of international isolation and fearful of a further imperialist invasion, symptoms of accommodation to bourgeois nationalist forces began to surface. A tendency to qualify political criticisms of the nationalists they supported militarily emerged. The Turkish regime's anti-working class measures began to be played down because of the supposed "objectively revolutionary role" it was playing. At the 12th Russian Communist Party Congress in April 1923 Bukharin declared that Turkey, "in spite of all persecutions of communists, plays a revolutionary role, since she is a destructive implement in relation to the imperialist system as a whole".[30] This hardly accorded with the resolution of the Second Comintern Congress:

> The Communist International has the duty of supporting the revolutionary movement in the colonies and backward countries only with the object of rallying the constituent elements of the future proletarian parties – which will be truly communist and not only in name – in all the backward countries and educating them to a consciousness of their special task, namely, that of fighting against the bourgeois-democratic trend in their nation.[31]

By 1924 the tendency to adapt to bourgeois nationalists was reflected in divisions among Turkish Communists. A right wing emerged that

29. Uzun 2004, p.197.
30. Carr 1966, p.479
31. Degras 1971, pp.143–44.

downplayed the importance of the workers' movement. The right called for support for Kemal so long as he fought "against imperialism and the remnants of the feudal system", implying he was actually doing both. In opposition to this approach the left argued to organise workers "against the bourgeoisie".[32] With the Stalinisation of the Comintern it was the right-wing opportunist line that won out. An alliance with the Turkish state was prioritised over workers' interests. By 1925 Turkish Communists were denouncing Kurdish rebellions against the Kemalist regime.

Iran

A second difficult test for the Bolshevik approach to national and social struggle in the semi-colonial world came in Iran (Persia as it was then called). Before World War I, while not strictly a colony, Iran had been divided into two spheres of influence: Russia the north, Britain the south. British capital dominated the oil industry. During the war British and Russian troops occupied Iran to forestall any German/ Turkish attempt to seize the oil industry. After the war Britain used Iran as a base to back the reactionary White Armies fighting Soviet Russia.

In a clear break with the imperialist policies of tsarism the Soviet government cancelled Iran's debts, renounced all the exploitative tsarist concessions and handed over to the Iranian government former Russian property.[33] This anti-imperialist approach, which sharply contrasted to Britain's ongoing manoeuvrings, led to a surge of popular enthusiasm for Soviet Russia among virtually all sections of the population and prevented the Iranian regime endorsing a proposed Anglo-Persian treaty.

The situation was complicated, however, by the formation in the northern province of Gilan of a quasi-independent nationalist government headed by Mirza Kuchak Khan. Kuchak Khan, whom the historian EH Carr describes as "part adventurer and part fanatic", was stridently anti-British and had probably received German subsidies.[34] By 1920 he was painting himself in Bolshevik colours. In May 1920 a

32. Carr 1972, p.656.
33. Carr 1966, p.243.
34. Carr 1966, pp.244–45.

strong Soviet force under the command of Fyodor Raskolnikov landed at Iran's Caspian Sea port of Enzeli to capture Russian ships abandoned by Denikin's retreating White Army. The Soviet forces linked up with Kuchak Khan, declaring an independent Soviet Republic. But some in Moscow were cautious about backing Kuchak Khan, who was no communist. They were more interested in influencing the Tehran government.

Previously in 1918 Iranian immigrant workers, inspired by the Russian revolution, had formed a Communist organisation, Adalat. Initially nationalist in orientation Adalat was radicalised by its participation in the Russian civil war and participated in the First Comintern Congress.[35] At its June 1920 Congress held in the Soviet Republic of Gilan the party was divided between a left "purely communist" faction, and a right "national revolutionary" faction. The right called for collaboration with Iranian capitalists and landlords, indeed that "no demonstrations should be tolerated against the landlords or the bourgeoisie". They argued: "all the revolutionary forces must be directed against the British. There can be no other tactic for us. Persia is not mature for Communism". The left, with initially a clear majority, called for the "sovietisation" of Persia along the lines followed by the Bolsheviks in Central Asia.[36] But under Soviet pressure the Iranian Central Committee declared in October 1920 that revolution in Iran would be possible only when full bourgeois development had been completed. This paved the way for the possibility of an alliance with the rising Iranian bourgeoisie against Britain.[37]

Russian courting of the Iranian government continued, despite a coup in February 1921 that brought the future Shah, Reza Khan, to power. By some accounts the Russian Consul, the former Menshevik Theodore Rothstein, who arrived in Tehran in April 1921, did not play a good role. He was criticised by Iranian Communists for being more interested in currying favour with the local elite than aiding the Communists.[38] Reza Khan, a modernising nationalist dictator hostile to the old feudal-style

35.   Chaqueri 2010, p.33.
36.   Chaqueri 2010, pp.34–36.
37.   Carr 1966, pp.292–93.
38.   Chaqueri 2010, pp.192–93.

regime, was an implacable opponent of the developing working-class movement and a relentless persecutor of communists. Nonetheless he received favourable coverage in the Soviet press as a "progressive".[39]

It was reasonable for the Soviet government to sign a treaty with Iran in February 1921. The withdrawal of support for the Gilan republic was also arguably justifiable. It is true that the Iranian working-class movement and the small Communist Party were in no position to challenge for power in the early 1920s. However from 1921 onwards Soviet policy in Iran was essentially emptied of revolutionary content. Strong national states on Russia's borders came to be seen as being in Russia's strategic interests. Consequently Reza Khan was courted and his government defended as a revolutionary nationalist opponent of imperialism. With the rise of Stalinism this opportunist bent became totally entrenched. As for the early Iranian Communist leaders, they were to suffer a terrible fate in the Stalinist purges of the 1930s – either shot outright or slowly dying in the concentration camps.[40]

Ireland: the missing revolutionary nationalist bourgeoisie

The issue of socialists attempting to identify the supposedly revolutionary nationalist section of the colonial bourgeoisie was nowhere more problematic than in Ireland. The most advanced section of the Irish bourgeoisie, Belfast's industrial capitalists, was tightly integrated into the British Empire. They bitterly opposed Irish nationalism and orchestrated the arming of Ulster's Protestant population to fight the introduction of Irish Home Rule. As for the economically weaker Dublin capitalists, for decades their ambitions never extended beyond Home Rule within the Empire. They condemned the physical force nationalists of the Irish Republican Brotherhood. The Dublin capitalists were terrified of revolt by workers and the rural poor and relied on the British state to suppress the subversive threat. The Home Rule capitalists' outlook was graphically demonstrated during the historic 1913 Dublin lock-out. Under the leadership of the notorious William Martin Murphy, Irish bosses worked hand in glove with the British authorities to brutally suppress an upsurge of working-class militancy

---

39. Carr 1972, pp.660–61.
40. Chaqueri 2010, pp.54–55.

spearheaded by the Irish Transport and General Workers' Union led by the revolutionary syndicalist James Larkin.

Yet by the end of World War I the Southern capitalists and their petty-bourgeois supporters seemingly had broken from their cautious stance. Abandoning support for the Home Rule party they threw their weight behind the Sinn Fein separatists and backed the Irish Republican Army (IRA) in the War of Independence. But this seeming shift to "revolutionary nationalism" and armed struggle to establish a republic was soon abandoned. Ever willing to compromise, in December 1921 the Southern capitalists endorsed a Treaty that denied full independence. Britain was allowed to retain part of the North while the South was to remain within the Empire as a so-called Free State. Highlighting the reality that there is no necessary correlation between support for armed struggle against colonial rule and political or social radicalism, IRA leader Michael Collins was a key proponent of the Treaty. Collins, a ruthless exponent of terror tactics against the British, was a conservative pro-capitalist nationalist who viewed the 1916 Easter Rebellion's proclamation of a Republic as "too socialistic". Collins, now armed by the British imperialists, built a Free State Army that crushed the anti-Treaty IRA in the subsequent Irish Civil War.

In the course of the War of Independence the reformist leaders of the Irish labour movement subordinated themselves to the nationalists. They accepted the dictum that "Labour must wait" until the national question was resolved. The union leaders endorsed the Free State and in the Civil War aligned with the Free State nationalists. "A major conse-quence of their denial of independent proletarian politics", as Mike Milotte writes, "was that most militant workers were absorbed into the republican melange".[41] This was a tragedy, as between 1917 and 1923 Ireland was rocked by working-class revolt, including three political general strikes. Aided by the breakdown of law and order during years of guerrilla warfare, there was an outburst of strikes and workplace occupations and the formation of local "soviets". In 1922 alone there were 80 workplace occupations. Workers flooded into the unions, and in a pathbreaking development agricultural workers won significant

---

41.   Milotte 1984, p.35.

gains in a surge of syndicalist militancy.[42] It was precisely because of the revolt from below that that the bourgeoisie sought to terminate the War of Independence. Had it gone on for longer there was a heightened possibility of it breaking out of the bounds of bourgeois nationalism and becoming a social struggle against capitalist rule.

In this context of immense challenges for socialists, Roddy Connolly, the son of British-executed socialist leader James Connolly, pushed to establish a Communist Party. Even for a party of many thousands with a crystal-clear approach to the national question it would not have been easy going. But this tiny group of never more than a hundred or so in its early years, which was far from clear politically, was set to be buffeted all over the place by mass forces. The young Communists' initial inclination was to concentrate on industrial militancy. Their 1920 report to the Second Comintern Congress downplayed the importance of the national question. "Taking a purely tactical view of nationalism, it described the IRA, as both 'potentially white guards' and fertile grounds for red propaganda".[43] Connolly fancifully argued that it would be easier to build a Communist Party among the Protestant workers of the North as they were less impacted by Irish nationalism. Consequently Ulster "may become one of the chief centres of the proletarian struggle against an Irish bourgeois state".[44]

Under the impact of the Second Comintern Congress discussion of the national question, Connolly and the other Irish delegate, Eadhmonn MacAlpine, ditched their previous approach and emphasised the national struggle. They declared: "Any force that tends to hinder the free play of the imperialist states against the developing world revolution must be encouraged and actively supported".[45] With Connolly reliant on Moscow for ideas, further flip-flops followed. In line with the Third Comintern Congress's slogan "To the Masses", Connolly next concentrated on trade union matters and the formation of Communist nuclei in unions and factories. The first issue of the

---

42. For an overview of the working-class rebellion see O'Connor 1988 and Kostick 1996.
43. O'Connor 2004, p.43.
44. Milotte 1984, p.53.
45. O'Connor 2004, p.44.

Communist Party of Ireland (CPI) paper, , did not mention the national struggle.

However with the signing of the Treaty in December 1921 the *Workers' Republic* editorial declared: "the people and fighters of Ireland must stand resolutely for de Valera and Brugha [anti-Treaty Republicans] – and this despite however reactionary either may be as regards the workers' aims".[46] Connolly believed the CPI was too small to influence the industrial revolt, but could make a breakthrough via an alliance with Republicans. During the Civil War the CPI operated as advisers to the Republicans, calling for them to orient to workers; advice the militarist IRA leaders happily ignored. The CPI abandoned the call for a workers' republic. But as Mike Milotte notes, "while urging support for the bourgeois republic the CPI did not attempt, even in a modest way, to prepare itself or the working class for an advance beyond that stage through the struggle for workers' power".[47] By mid-1922 the Comintern was moving towards a two-stage revolution approach, declaring: "It is only after the yoke of the English imperialists has been shaken off that the struggle against the Irish exploiters will have any chance of success!"[48] By 1923 Connolly and other leading CPI members had accepted jobs as Sinn Fein organisers. The initial CPI was wound up on 26 January 1924.

Yet for all the confusions of the early Communists they were not simply Stalin's creatures. They had their own independent minds and by the late 1920s they had been driven out of the movement. From then on the leaders of Irish Communism were Moscow-trained hacks. These Stalinist leaders backed all the twists and turns coming out of Russia. By the popular front years of the mid-1930s, Irish Communists had fully embraced the two-stage theory, leaving the struggle for socialism to a distant future. They voted down the call from the left wing of the Republican Congress for a workers' republic. This class-collaborationist approach led them to support Fianna Fail, the dominant party of Irish capitalism, for the next 60 years.

---

46.   O'Connor 2004, p.57.
47.   Milotte 1984, p.56.
48.   O'Connor 2004, p.64.

China 1925–27: a decisive test

By 1925 China was in ferment. Workers were on the move in the big cities and in the countryside peasants were seizing the land.[49] The young Chinese Communist Party (CCP) was growing rapidly, but could it make the most of the revolutionary opportunities? The First Congress in July 1921 of the then very small CCP outlined the following program:

> A. With the revolutionary army of the proletariat to overthrow the capitalistic classes, to reconstruct the nation from the labour class, until class distinctions are eliminated.

> B. To adopt the dictatorship of the proletariat in order to complete the end of class struggle – abolishing the classes.

> C. To overthrow the private ownership of capital, to confiscate all the productive means...and to entrust them to social ownership.

> D. To unite with the Third International.[50]

However under concerted pressure from the Comintern this approach of fighting for working-class rule was gradually abandoned. Instead the Communists submitted themselves to the authority of the bourgeois-nationalist Guomindang (GMD[51]). By 1925 the CCP stood for limiting the revolution to achieving a bourgeois republic. This left the CCP theoretically and politically compromised. Lacking a clear perspective of fighting for a soviet government, the whole logic of the situation meant that the Communists were pushed in the direction of tailing along behind the GMD. The CCP ended up playing a similar role to that of the Mensheviks in Russia in 1917, which blocked with the bourgeois Kadets and opposed workers taking power. Consequently the revolutionary wave that swept China went down to a crushing defeat. The Communists were massacred and driven from the cities.

---

49. For the 1925–27 Chinese revolution see Isaacs 2009, Bramble and Armstrong 2021, chapter 7 and Pantsov 2000.
50. Pantsov 2000, p.36.
51. Known at the time as the Kuomintang.

It was not a question of misguided but well-meaning advice coming from Moscow. The bureaucratic degeneration of the Russian revolution and the cynical opportunist policies pursued by the Comintern from 1924 onwards, first under Zinoviev's leadership and then under Bukharin/Stalin, made the situation for the Chinese Communists far worse. The CCP's original entry into the GMD, though imposed rather bureaucratically by the Comintern, was possibly justifiable. Indeed Trotsky continued to defend that decision:

> The participation of the CCP in the Guomindang was perfectly correct in the period when the CCP was a propaganda society that was only preparing itself for future *independent* political activity but which, at the same time, sought to take part in the ongoing national liberation struggles.[52]

There is, however, a sharp distinction between working inside the GMD to build up the revolutionary forces and subordinating Communists to bourgeois nationalists. By 1926 subordination to the nationalists was precisely the line from Moscow, even though the GMD was cracking down on the working-class movement. In the face of desperate pleas from the CCP leadership to break with the nationalists and be given Russian arms to defend themselves, the CCP was forbidden from fomenting seizures of land by the peasantry and from campaigning against the Chinese bourgeoisie, as this "would weaken the fighting capacity of the Guomindang".[53] Stalin's chief emissary in China, Borodin, put it bluntly: "The present period is one in which the Communists should do coolie service for the Kuomintang".[54]

Previously, in January 1926, the Russian party greeted the GMD's Congress with the message: "To our Party has fallen the proud and historic role of leading the first victorious proletarian revolution of the world… We are convinced that the Kuomintang will succeed in playing the same role in the East".[55] Soon afterwards the GMD was admitted to

52. Trotsky 1976, p.114.
53. Pantsov 2000, p.94.
54. Hallas 1985, p.120.
55. Harris 1978, p.9.

the Communist International as a sympathising party! In October 1926 Trotsky summed up the fatal weakness of the Stalinist policy:

> The Chinese bourgeoisie is sufficiently realistic and acquainted intimately enough with the nature of world imperialism to understand that a really serious struggle against the latter requires such an upheaval of the revolutionary masses as would primarily become a menace to the bourgeoisie itself... And if we taught the workers of Russia from the very beginning not to believe in the readiness of liberalism and the ability of petit-bourgeois democracy to crush tsarism and to destroy feudalism, we should no less energetically imbue the Chinese workers from the outset with the same spirit of distrust. The new and absolutely false theory promulgated by Stalin-Bukharin about the "immanent" revolutionary spirit of the colonial bourgeoisie is, in substance the translation of Menshevism into the language of Chinese politics.[56]

The Chinese Communists were undoubtedly heroic fighters. On numerous occasions they argued against the directives coming from an increasingly Stalinist-dominated Comintern. But the Chinese Communists did not have an alternative theoretical perspective of maintaining working-class independence from bourgeois nationalist forces in order to carry the struggle against imperialism beyond the bourgeois stage into a struggle for soviet power. They were not helped by the fact that Trotsky did not generalise his theory of permanent revolution to China until some years into the revolutionary process. Consequently the CCP equivocated. And if you are not politically prepared to push the struggle all the way, to break decisively with the nationalists and challenge for power, you are bound to be defeated. In the Chinese case it proved to be at an enormous cost.

---

56. Trotsky 1976, p.297.

Drawing the lessons

In 1920 or 1924 principled revolutionaries could have a genuine debate about whether the social forces existed for socialist revolutions in the colonial and semi-colonial world. There were vast differences in economic development between India and China at one extreme and Saudi Arabia and Laos at the other. This is simply not the reality of world capitalism today. In the case of the Middle East the working class currently forms a much greater percentage of the population than in Russia in 1917, and the level of economic development is far higher. The Arab Spring of 2011 confirmed that there is enormous potential for social revolt.

Leon Trotsky drew important lessons from the defeat of the Chinese revolution, arguing for the application of the theory of permanent revolution more generally to the colonial world. In 1932 he wrote in the chapter "The Problem of Nationalities", in his seminal *History of the Russian Revolution*:

> This appraisal of national wars and revolutions does not by any means imply, however, that the bourgeoisie of the colonial and semi-colonial nations have a revolutionary mission. On the contrary, this bourgeoisie of backward countries from the days of its milk teeth grows up as an agentry of foreign capital, and notwithstanding its envious hatred of foreign capital, always does and always will in every decisive situation turn up in the same camp with it. Chinese compradorism is the classic form of the colonial bourgeoisie, and the Kuomintang is the classic party of compradorism. The upper circles of the petty bourgeoisie, including the intelligentsia, may take an active and occasionally a very noisy part in the national struggles, but they are totally incapable of playing an independent role. Only the working class standing at the head of the nation can carry either a national or an agrarian revolution clear through.[57]

Tragically it was too late to change the Communist parties' political

---

57.   Trotsky 1997, p.908.

orientation. By the early 1930s they were thoroughly Stalinised and were no longer a revolutionary factor. For the Comintern, workers' revolutions in colonial countries were now totally off the agenda. Indeed they were to be sabotaged. The Comintern turned support for bourgeois nationalist forces in countries like China, which they hoped would ally with Russia, into a reactionary dogma. The Stalinists covered up this counter-revolutionary policy with the pathetic gloss of a supposed second socialist stage of the colonial revolt at some point in the distant future. Hand in hand with fighting to limit revolts in the colonies to just setting up a bourgeois state came the policy of class alliances with so-called progressive sections of the capitalist class, petty-bourgeois nationalists and even at times landlords. Defeat after defeat for the working-class movement followed, from Iraq to Iran to Indonesia and Palestine.

Deflected permanent revolution

In the decades after World War II the great bulk of former colonies and semi-colonies achieved their formal independence. In some cases, such as Algeria, Indonesia, Mozambique and Vietnam, the colonial power was defeated and driven out, but in a number of other cases, including Nigeria, Jordan, Papua New Guinea, Botswana and Fiji, the colonial power withdrew, despite facing only limited popular rebellion. In no case did the working class win the leadership of the national movement and carry the struggle for national independence over into a struggle for socialism.

How can we explain this major shift? In part it reflected a radically changed balance of imperial power. The United States had cemented itself economically and militarily as the overwhelmingly dominant imperialist power. The colonial rule of the old imperialist powers of Britain, France and the Netherlands over vast swathes of Africa and Asia was an obstacle to the economic penetration and profit-making possibilities of US companies. The US did not feel the need to replace the old colonial regime with a direct US colonial administration. In most cases US economic power, backed up by the occasional military intervention or CIA-backed coup to put the "right" people in power, was considered sufficient and a far cheaper way to rule the world.

Where major anti-colonial struggles did occur it was neither the local bourgeoisie nor the working class that led the national liberation movement to victory. Instead sections of the intelligentsia and the middle class linked to the old colonial state apparatus and the military played the decisive leading role. The working class was unable to play a decisive revolutionary role in a swathe of countries because of the counter-revolutionary politics of the Stalinist Communist parties. National independence was obtained but the working class and the peasant masses in no sense achieved their social freedom. Instead, in a process British Marxist Tony Cliff dubbed "deflected permanent revolution", authoritarian statified regimes were established either by nationalist parties in Algeria, Syria, Egypt and Iraq or by Stalinist Communist parties in China, North Korea and Vietnam.[58] Trotsky's previously quoted 1932 statement that the "upper circles of the petty bourgeoisie, including the intelligentsia...are totally incapable of playing an independent role" was proved wrong.[59]

These developments in the colonial world underline the fact that nothing is inevitable in human history. There is not some automatic process that propels the working class into the leadership of the struggle for national independence. As Trotsky himself had previously noted in 1927, "the bourgeois tasks can be resolved in various ways".[60] Revolutionaries can't rely on "great social forces" to do the job for them. Human intervention is necessary and that means the construction of a mass revolutionary working-class party that determinedly fights to win the leadership of the movement for national and social liberation.

The appalling story of Stalinism in the Middle East

The role of the Communist parties in the Middle East was particularly egregious. Prior to the 1930s the Arab Communist parties were tiny. In the early 1930s the original Communist leaders, who were genuine working-class revolutionaries, were purged and the parties Stalinised. New leaders trained in Moscow loyally carried out the dictates of Russian foreign policy – the policy of the counter-revolutionary regime

---

58.   Cliff 1963.
59.   Trotsky 1997, p.908.
60.   Trotsky 1976, p.163.

that had destroyed workers' power. The last thing Russia's rulers wanted were workers' revolutions that would threaten their imperialist interests. For Stalin and Co. the role of Arab Communists was to find allies for Russia. From the mid-1930s onwards Moscow directed Communists to embrace a popular front policy that subordinated the interests of workers and peasants to the supposedly progressive national bourgeoisie. In 1943 Syrian Communist leader Khalid Bakdash emphasised that the party's goal was not socialism but simply independence and cross class national unity. Bakdash assured

> the national capitalist, the national factory owner, that we do not look with envy or with malice on his national enterprise. On the contrary, we desire his progress and vigorous growth... We assure the owner of land that we do not and shall not demand the confiscation of his property... All we ask is kindness towards the peasant.[61]

The popular front's precise form varied over time. The section of the bourgeoisie that was lauded as progressive could change dramatically overnight. During World War II Moscow told Communists to back the war effort of Stalin's British ally. Consequently Communists opposed strikes. Bourgeois forces that continued to campaign against British colonialism went, in the eyes of the Stalinists, from being progressive allies to outright fascists. Later the main task was to curry favour with the new nationalist regimes. Moscow spelt it out in 1960:

> At the head of the majority of new national states...stand bourgeois political leaders... this cannot belittle the progressive historical importance of the breakthrough that has taken place... the central task...remains for a comparatively long period of time that of struggle not against capital but against survivals of the Middle Ages. From this stems the possibility of the cooperation over a long period of the workers, peasants and intelligentsia... with that part of the national bourgeoisie which is interested

---

61. Ismael and Ismael 1998, pp.32–33.

in the independent political and economic development of its country and is ready to defend its independence against any encroachments by the imperialist powers.[62]

Popular front politics had an incredibly damaging impact on the working-class movement. In Iraq, following the popular revolution of July 1958 that overthrew the monarchy, the Communists built up powerful working-class support, led the student movement, established its own security force and won influence in the army. On a series of occasions the Communists mobilised hundreds of thousands onto the streets of Baghdad, Basra and other cities. By 1959 the CP was in a position to challenge for power. But under pressure from Moscow the Iraqi CP leadership refused to break with the nationalist government of General Qasim, the supposed representative of the national bourgeoisie.[63] Despite intensified repression of the workers' movement, and in defiance of pressure from their rank and file for a determined stance, the Communists continued to hail Qasim as the "sole leader" and a "true son of the people". Party activity in the army was frozen. The failure to mobilise workers to fight for power led to a crushing defeat. As the Iraqi CP admitted some years later:

> We let slip through our fingers a historic opportunity and allowed a squandering of a unique revolutionary situation... after the defeat of the Mosul conspiracy Qasim had found himself in a tight spot... Our party became, in effect, the master of the situation... and should have gone on to conquer power... To say the masses, loving Qasim, would have stood against us is untrue... Had we seized the helm and without delay armed the people, carried out a radical agrarian reform, granted to the Kurds their autonomy and, by revolutionary measures, transformed the army into a democratic force, our regime would have with extraordinary speed attained to the widest popularity and would have released

---

62. Birchall 1974, pp.99–100.
63. Batatu 1978, p.903.

great mass initiatives, enabling the millions to make their own history.[64]

By the time Qasim himself was overthrown by the Ba'ath party in a CIA-backed coup the Communists were in a far weakened position. At least five thousand Communists were murdered and thousands more rounded up from their jobs and carried off to prison by the lorry load.[65] The Communists learned nothing from this disaster. In the 1970s the Iraqi CP took cabinet posts in the authoritarian Ba'athist government until Saddam Hussein had them hanged.

Lebanon and Palestine

There are stark lessons from the Lebanese civil war of the 1970s and 1980s for the Palestinian cause and the broader Arab world today.[66] Communists played a prominent role during the radical wave of struggle by workers, students and peasants that led up to the civil war and during the armed struggle. They had a following that cut across Lebanon's entrenched communal and sectarian lines. The Lebanese Communist Party (LCP) and the Organisation of Communist Action both had Christian leaders yet won a Shiite following. The Organisation of Communist Action in particular grew rapidly, gaining strong support among Shiites in the South and in Beirut's suburbs. Communist leaders belonged to the inner decision-making circle of the left and nationalist alliance. They were close to the central leader of the movement – Druze leader and head of the Progressive Socialist Party Kamil Jumblatt. But their approach was not to push the struggle forward to challenge the foundations of Lebanese capitalism. Instead the LCP's fourth congress called for the creation of a broad alliance of all the forces that wanted to maintain Lebanon as a "united, independent, sovereign, free, Arab democratic country, regardless of their class origins, ideological differences, religious or sectarian affiliations, positions inside or outside authority, and differences of political views".[67]

---

64. Batatu 1978, p.904.
65. Birchall 1974, pp.101–3.
66. For an overview of the Lebanese civil war see Petran 1987.
67. Ismael and Ismael 1998, p.110.

The Communists did not advance a program of substantial reforms to improve workers' living standards. They limited themselves to measures to modernise the superstructure of Lebanese capitalism.[68] Despite the Communists militarily controlling some of Beirut's largest suburbs, the left did not organise democratic control of these areas. This approach was self-defeating. It served to undermine the masses' sense of ownership over the struggle and weaken their fighting capacity. The left conducted the civil war as a military battle, not a social revolt that could galvanise all the popular masses, including the large numbers of Maronite Christian workers and poor peasants, to fight for their liberation. The almost exclusive emphasis on nationalist resistance to the Israelis and their fascist Lebanese allies opened the left and the Palestinian resistance up to isolation. This was graphically demonstrated in the aftermath the 1982 Israeli invasion of Lebanon. The communalist Amal organisation, with the backing of the Syrian regime, mobilised sections of the Shiite population against the Palestinians and the left, whom they blamed for the devastation wreaked by Israeli attacks. Amal aped the Lebanese fascists of the Phalange with its own massacres of Palestinians.

The radical potential of this great social upheaval was squashed. The vicious sectarian social order that was Lebanese capitalism was preserved. Sectarianism became more pronounced. The defeat of the left-wing challenge shattered hopes for change. Growing economic difficulties and immense corruption led to widespread emigration and increased dependence on the patronage of sectarian political bosses who gained power and wealth by dispensing largesse and political favours.

The defeat of the left was not simply due to the US-backed invasion of Lebanon by Assad's Syrian regime in 1976. To understand why this tremendous social explosion during the 1960s and 1970s did not end in a successful socialist revolution you need to critically examine the politics of the key radical currents. The main military force, the Yasser Arafat-led Palestine Liberation Organisation (PLO), adhered to a nationalist program that sought to win a capitalist Palestinian state.

---

68.   Traboulsi 2007, pp.189 and 203.

It advocated a combination of guerrilla struggle and alliances with Arab regimes. The PLO leadership opposed a strategy of mass social mobilisations as that would threaten not just the Zionist state but the Arab ruling classes. So while the PLO defended itself when attacked by the right, it was always looking for a compromise.

To the left of the PLO were the Communists and groups such as the Popular Front for the Liberation of Palestine (PFLP), which called itself Marxist-Leninist. A Communist Party of Lebanon and Syria was founded in Beirut in 1924 by a group of workers and intellectuals inspired by the workers' revolution in Russia. In July 1925 an uprising against colonial rule swept Syria and Lebanon. The French responded with ruthless repression. Police opened fire on a Communist-organised demonstration in Beirut, killing 10 and wounding 40. The CP leadership was arrested and the party broken. In the early 1930s the CP revived and, working underground, built strong support among tobacco workers, electricity workers, waterfront workers and tram workers.

But in the mid-1930s, rather than mobilise workers against French rule, the Communists were told by Moscow to soft-pedal their opposition to imperialism and establish a popular front of middle-class and bourgeois forces. Then in 1947 they were instructed to back the setting up of the Israeli state, which Moscow saw as a potential ally. This had a disastrous impact on Communist parties throughout the Arab world. The joint Communist Party of Syria and Lebanon, which had built up substantial support during a postwar strike wave, saw its membership collapse from 18,000 in 1947 to just a few hundred. Dissidents who opposed the pro-Zionist line were expelled. Consequently Communists were in no position to take advantage of the wave of strikes and protests that rocked Syria after the failure of the Arab regimes to defend Palestine.[69] Despite repeated failures, popular front-style class-collaborationist politics, rather than clear-cut class politics, remained hegemonic in one form or another on the Arab left for decades.

In Palestine the popular front approach meant that in the Arab revolt of 1936–39 the Palestine Communist Party (PCP) was unable to offer a class-struggle alternative to the reactionary Arab leadership of

---

69.   Ismael and Ismael 1998, pp.38–39.

landlords, clerics and bourgeois forces. And because the PCP effectively abandoned class politics for nationalism it was in a weaker position to hold the line against Zionist nationalism among its Jewish worker members (a majority of members in the 1930s). The end result was the formation of two Communist parties in British Mandate Palestine. One party, predominantly Jewish in composition, tailed Zionism. The other party, predominantly Palestinian in composition, tailed Arab nationalism.

Russia's support for setting up the Israeli state in 1948 discredited Communists for many years, especially among Palestinians driven from their land. Consequently the new Palestinian left that developed in the 1960s, the Popular Front for the Liberation of Palestine (PFLP) and the Democratic Front for the Liberation of Palestine (DFLP), were not direct descendants of the old PCP. The official Communist Party did retain some influence among Arabs within Israel, but it was a reformist party committed to the Zionist state. And the PCP on the West Bank was a conservative force promoting a two-state solution.

The tragedy was that when new forces emerging out of the 1960s radical wave groped towards Marxism the predominant ideas on offer on the international left, and even more so in the Middle East, were still those of Stalinism. The PFLP and DFLP ended up embracing a popular front-style approach, as reflected in the names of the organisations. The new Palestinian left developed within the Arab National Movement (ANM), which originated among a group of intellectuals at the American University of Beirut, the most prominent of which were George Habash and Wadie Haddad. The ANM had an elitist approach of armed struggle by small bands of guerrillas. They saw their armed actions as a means to pressure the Arab states to launch a war on Israel. In its early years the ANM was conservative politically and, reflecting their leaders' upper middle-class social backgrounds, hostile to working-class politics, which they saw as disrupting Arab national unity.

The crushing defeat of the Arab armies in the 1967 war with Israel discredited the nationalist regimes and the ANM began to look to the Vietnamese model of a "protracted people's war". In December 1967 George Habash established the PFLP, based on a version of Stalinised

Marxism looking to Cuba and China. Then in February 1969 the Democratic Front split from the PFLP. Initially the Democratic Front, influenced by New Left ideas and with a following among Palestinian students in Europe and the US, was the more leftish and open group. Some Palestinian Trotskyists exiled in Europe joined.

The Democratic Front rejected Arab chauvinism (and slogans such as drive the Jews into the sea, still influential in the 1960s) and placed less emphasis on militarism than the PFLP, which in 1969/1970 engaged in plane hijackings. The Democratic Front called for the "establishment of a democratic state in which Arabs and Jews shall enjoy equal national rights and responsibilities" as part of a federal socialist state of the whole region. It sought links with the Israeli Trotskyist group Matzpen.[70] In 1970 during the mass upheavals in Jordan both the DFLP and the PFLP called for all power to the resistance and a socialist state.[71] But after the Jordanian state crushed the resistance the DFLP moved to the right, purging its left wing and adopting a pro-Moscow orientation. During the Lebanese civil war the DFLP, which had previously been critical of the PLO's failure to launch an all-out struggle against the far right, dropped out of the fighting once Russia's ally Syria invaded Lebanon. The main game for Moscow was its relationship with regimes like Syria. That meant that the interests of Arab and Palestinian Communists were always sacrificed. The Russians were also keen to develop a relationship with Fatah, the mainstream PLO leadership, to which from the late 1970s they gave substantial funding and arms. Consequently a strong pro-Moscow Stalinist current developed within Fatah.

The DFLP began to popularise the idea of a Palestinian mini-state in the Occupied Territories. Much of the Fatah leadership supported a mini-state but faced opposition within their ranks so were happy for the DFLP to be the stalking horse. The DFLP was smaller than the PFLP, with less of a base in the refugee camps, but it had an ideological impact on left-wing intellectual circles. In the early 1970s it published an influential weekly paper in Beirut with the Lebanese Communist Action Organisation. This enabled it to play an important

---

70. Fiedler 2022, pp.224–25.
71. Marshall 1989, pp.124–26.

role in rallying sections of the secular Arab intelligentsia to support a two-state position. It was a slippery slope. The end result was that the DFLP became little more than a left cover for Fatah's betrayals.

The PFLP was hostile to "Arab reaction", represented in its view by feudalism and capitalism – the rulers of Kuwait, Saudi Arabia, the Gulf States and Jordan. It was less critical of supposedly radical regimes – Algeria, South Yemen, Syria, Libya and at times Iraq. Indeed George Habash attacked the DFLP as suffering from "infantile leftism" because of its harsh criticisms of the nationalist regimes. But the nationalist governments were far from reliable allies of the Palestinian masses. Their approach was not qualitatively different from that of Jordan or Saudi Arabia. By tying themselves to these regimes the PFLP downplayed the need to build a mass revolutionary movement from below throughout the Arab world. The PFLP ended up providing a left cover for regimes like the Ba'ath in Iraq and Syria. So while the PFLP talked a lot about the role of the masses and the working class, this became little more than a rhetorical incantation as it sought alliances with various non-proletarian forces. In 1970 Habash went to China to win support and China began to send the PFLP considerable amounts of arms. This came at a cost, as the Chinese opposed the PFLP's attacks on conservative Arab regimes with which China was trying to curry favour.

Despite all sorts of tensions the PFLP refused to break with the Fatah-dominated PLO. The PFLP called for national unity of all Palestinian groups. In other words, despite declaring itself a Marxist-Leninist organisation, it consistently put nation before class. The PFLP did not want to disrupt national unity and sought to unite with the bourgeois-dominated Fatah rather than build a class-struggle alternative to Fatah's betrayals of workers and peasants. Eventually the PFLP toned down its opposition to a two-state solution, and when the Palestinian Authority was established chose to operate within its frame-work. The failure of the PFLP, the DFLP and the official Communist parties to build a class-struggle alternative to Fatah demoralised their supporters. The demoralisation was compounded by the collapse of the Russian bloc, which the Arab left had mistakenly looked to as socialist. This opened up space for the Islamists, who cohered a new generation of Palestinians who wanted to fight. But the Islamists were incapable of offering a road forward and just like Fatah led the Palestinian people down the road to further defeats.

A new revolutionary left needs to be built in Palestine and across the Arab world. A left that bases itself on a clear rejection of alliances with, let alone subordination to, capitalist forces. A left that puts working-class unity ahead of national unity. A left that has no truck with any of the Arab regimes, whether so called progressive or reactionary. A left that fights for working-class leadership of the struggle against Zionism and imperialism. A left that seeks to rally the urban poor, the peasantry and the Palestinian refugees behind the working class and recognises that ultimately freedom for the Palestinian people can only be won by a socialist revolution that sweeps away the Zionist state and the bourgeois Arab states.

The limitations of the democratic secular state demand

Talk of a two-state solution for the Palestinian people has long been a fraud promoted by the US and other Western governments, including Australia, to cover up Israel's ongoing colonial expansionism. The Israelis are determined to establish facts on the ground to prevent any possibility of a Palestinian state being established alongside Israel. They won't even tolerate a pathetic mini-state on the West Bank and Gaza.

So what is the solution for the Palestinian people? Many on the left, who rightly reject the nonsense of a two-state solution, have called for a democratic secular state across the whole of historic Palestine. This was the position that Socialist Alternative long supported. However the democratic secular state demand is in reality a call for a bourgeois national state. That was the standpoint of Fatah, the key force that originally popularised it in the 1970s. It was a demand tailored to serve the interests of the Palestinian capitalist class, which wanted to establish a state that they ruled over. There was nothing ambiguous about it. Many of us on the left believed that fighting for a democratic secular state would challenge capitalism. We were mistaken. There was nothing transitional about the demand for a democratic secular state. It did not go beyond the framework of capitalism. Limiting the Palestinian struggle for freedom to simply a capitalist state led to setback after setback, from Black September in Jordan in 1970 to Lebanon during its wave of revolt across the 1970s. When Fatah's strategy of guerrilla struggle proved incapable of defeating Israel they settled for ruling over a mini-state that policed the Palestinian population on behalf of US imperialism and the Zionists. If the movement for Palestinian freedom does not break with the ruling classes of the Arab states and with the Palestinian capitalist class and the various petty-bourgeois nationalists there is no way out.

Socialist Alternative has long recognised that the Palestinian working class, divided between those workers within the confines of the Israeli state, those on the West Bank and Gaza and the refugees in Jordan, Syria and Lebanon, does not have the power on its own to overthrow the Zionist state. The Palestinian masses desperately need allies. Those potential allies do exist among the workers of the region. Socialist revolutions that overthrow the capitalist Arab regimes would have the capacity to go on to challenge imperialism and the Zionist state. But why call for socialist revolutions in Egypt, Algeria, Tunisia, Jordan and Iraq but not in Palestine?

Advocating a socialist revolution to liberate Palestine does not mean that Marxists entirely rule out the possibility of some sort of Palestinian state being established short of socialism. Though anything more than some prettified version of the current West Bank mini-state is highly unlikely under capitalism. Yet plenty of unexpected things have happened in history. Both World War I and World War II tore up old empires and saw numerous new states carved out. It is impossible to predict the international ramifications of a major imperialist war between the US and China. But socialists need to champion the best possible outcome for workers and the oppressed, not leave it to the machinations of the imperialist powers or petty-bourgeois nationalist forces.

Nor does calling for a socialist revolution to liberate Palestine mean abandoning more immediate demands. Socialists need to champion a range of specific demands, such as ending the siege on Gaza, ending Israeli settlements on the West Bank, the release of political prisoners and the right of return of Palestinian refugees. In the West today socialists' campaigning should focus on the right of the Palestinian people to fight for their national freedom. Socialists also campaign to expose the role of their own governments and US imperialism and attempt to build a solidarity movement. However, more than that we fight to build a socialist movement to challenge the imperialist system in its heartlands. To do that most effectively socialists need to have an overall strategic view of how Palestinian national and social liberation can be achieved. Socialists can't afford to tail along behind the various nationalist currents.

An overall strategic view of advocating socialist revolution in the Arab world, and in particular Palestine, is even more important for socialists in the Middle East. If there is to be any hope of victory for the Palestinian people, a powerful revolutionary movement that challenges the various bourgeois and petty-bourgeois nationalists as well as the Islamists needs to be built in Egypt and the other Arab states, and very importantly in Palestine itself. Otherwise the heroic struggles of the Palestinian people will continue to face defeat after defeat.

Conclusion

How can the devastating cycle of imperialist invasions, genocide, exploitation and authoritarian rule that has been inflicted on the people of the Middle East be ended? There is profound sympathy among workers and the poor of the Arab world for the Palestinian cause, but the brutal dictators who rule Egypt, Saudi Arabia and Jordan have so far been able to hold it in check popular mobilisations. There is a burning need for a socialist left that can galvanise the masses into action. The Arab Spring revolutions that swept the region just over a decade ago showed the potential for rebellion against these detested regimes. But today the region's once powerful left is very weak because of the disastrous failure of the class-collaborationist Stalinist politics that long dominated the socialist movement. The mass of workers and urban poor have the capacity to overthrow the hold of imperialism, the Zionist state and their local rulers. But to achieve that objective demands the construction of a new revolutionary left which breaks with the nationalist and Stalinist tradition that has so blighted the Arab left and instead sets its sights on workers' self-emancipation.

References

Armstrong, Mick 2016, "Nestor Makhno: the failure of anarchism", *Marxist Left Review*, 12, Winter. https://marxistleftreview.org/?issue-number=12

Batatu, Hanna 1978, *The Old Social Classes and the Revolutionary Movements of Iraq*, Princeton University Press.

Birchall, Ian 1974, *Workers against the Monolith*, Pluto Press.

Bramble, Tom and Mick Armstrong 2021, *The Fight for Workers' Power. Revolution and Counter-Revolution in the 20th Century*, Interventions.

Bukharin, Nikolai and Evgenii Preobrazhensky 1920, *The ABC of Communism* (chapter 6). https://www.marxists.org/archive/bukharin/works/1920/abc/06.htm#046

Carr, EH 1966, *The Bolshevik Revolution 1917–1923*, Vol. 3, Penguin Books.

Carr, EH 1972, *Socialism in One Country 1924–1926*, Vol. 3, Penguin Books.

Chaqueri, Cosroe (ed.) 2010, "The Left in Iran, 1905–1940", *Revolutionary History*, 10 (2), Merlin Press.

Cliff, Tony 1963, *"Deflected Permanent Revolution"*, *International Socialism*, 1:12, Spring. https://www.marxists.org/archive/cliff/works/1963/xx/permrev.htm

Degras, Jane (ed.) 1971, *The Communist International 1919–1943. Documents*, Vol. 1, Frank Cass.

Draper, Hal 1969, *The ABC of National Liberation Movements*. https://www.marxists.org/archive/draper/1969/abc/index.htm

Evans, Les and Russell Block (eds) 1976, *Leon Trotsky on China*, Monad Press.

Fiedler, Lutz 2020, *Matzpen. A History of Israeli Dissidence*, Edinburgh University Press.

Geier, Joel 2024, "Socialist Alternatives: The Portuguese Revolution", *Marxist Left Review*, 27, Autumn. https://marxistleftreview.org/?issue-number=27

Hallas, Duncan 1985, *The Comintern*, Bookmarks.

Hallas, Duncan 2003, *Trotsky's Marxism*, Haymarket Books.

Harris, Nigel 1978, *The Mandate of Heaven: Marx and Mao in Modern China*, Quartet.

Harris, Nigel 1992, *National Liberation*, Penguin Books.

Isaacs, Harold 2010, *The Tragedy of the Chinese Revolution*, Haymarket Books.

Kostick, Conor 1996, *Revolution in Ireland. Popular Militancy 1917 to 1923*, Pluto Press.

Lenin, VI 1912, "Democracy and Narodism in China", *Collected Works*, Vol. 18, Progress Publishers.

Lenin, VI 1914, "The Right of Nations to Self-Determination", *Collected Works*, Vol. 20, Progress Publishers.

Lenin, VI 1916, "The discussion on self-determination summed up", *Collected Works*, Vol. 22, Progress Publishers.

Lynch, David 2005, *Radical Politics in Modern Ireland. The Irish Socialist Republican Party 1896–1904*, Irish Academic Press.

Marshall, Phil 1989, *Intifada. Zionism, imperialism and Palestinian resistance*, Bookmarks.

Marx, Karl *and Frederick Engels* 1989, *Collected Works*, Vol. 43, *Correspondence 1868–70*, International Publishers.

Milotte, Mike 1984, *Communism in Modern Ireland: The Pursuit of the Workers' Republic since 1916*, Gill and Macmillan.

O'Connor, Emmet 1988, *Syndicalism in Ireland 1917–1923*, Cork University Press.

O'Connor, Emmet 2004, *Reds and the Green. Ireland, Russia and the Communist Internationals 1919–43*, University College Dublin Press.

Pantsov, Alexander 2000, *The Bolsheviks and the Chinese Revolution 1919–1927*, University of Hawai'i Press.

Petran, Tabitha 1987, *The Struggle over Lebanon*, Monthly Review Press.

Riddell, John (ed.) 1984, *Lenin's Struggle for a Revolutionary International. Documents 1907–1916. The Preparatory Years*, Monad Press.

Riddell, John (ed.) 1987, *Founding the Communist International. Proceedings and Documents of the First Congress, March 1919*, Pathfinder Press.

Riddell, John (ed.) 1993, *To See the Dawn. Baku, 1920 First Congress of the Peoples of the East*, Pathfinder Press.

Riddell, John (ed.) 2012, *Toward the United Front. Proceedings of the Fourth Congress of the Communist International, 1922*, Haymarket Books.

Second Congress of the Communist International, *Minutes of the Proceedings*, Vol. 1, 1977, New Park.

Traboulsi, Fawwaz 2007, *A History of Modern Lebanon*, Pluto Press.

Trotsky, Leon 1969, *The Permanent Revolution and Results and Prospects*, Pathfinder Press.

Trotsky, Leon 1976, *Leon Trotsky on China*, Monad Press.

Trotsky, Leon 1997, *The History of the Russian Revolution*, Pluto Press.

Uzum, Cem 2004, *Making the Turkish Revolution*, antikapitalist.

VASHTI FOX

The rise and fall of the Palestinian Fronts

Vashti Fox was a founder of Students for Palestine and has written numerous articles on Palestine, Zionism and the Middle East. She has also been a leading activist in anti-fascist campaigns.

O N 6 SEPTEMBER 1970, a young couple travelling under Honduran passports boarded an El Al Boeing 707 flight to Amsterdam. Seated in the second row of the tourist class section of the plane bound for New York, they were well dressed and calm. In fact, the passengers were in disguise. The man, Patrick Arguello, was a Nicaraguan-American member of the Sandinista movement. The woman, Leila Khaled, was a notorious figure in the Palestinian liberation movement. Khaled had grenades in her handbag and Arguello a pistol in his trousers. As the plane headed over the English Channel, the couple tried to force their way into the cockpit. At the same time, across Europe and the Middle East, several other planes were being hijacked and diverted to a place called Dawson's Field, a defunct British RAF base in Jordan renamed Revolution Field. This operation was launched by an organisation called the Popular Front for the Liberation of Palestine (PFLP).

The Amsterdam operation went badly wrong. The pilot nosedived the plane, throwing the hijackers off kilter, and the plane guards shot and killed Patrick Arguello. Khaled was arrested by British authorities and kept for over a month in a London prison, during which time she became a media sensation. The hijackings were front page news of the global press for weeks. This and several previous hijackings were some of the most high-profile actions of the PFLP during this period. The grounding of the hijacked planes and their hostages in Jordan reflected the growing size and implantation of various new armed Palestinian resistance groups in the country. Indeed, their size and growing confidence precipitated the eventual brutal crackdown by the Jordanian monarchy on the Palestinian movement in 1970.

Khaled later justified the hijackings in the following statement:

> In all my time, in all my statements, I always said we were forced to do it. It wasn't because we liked to do it, we knew beforehand that those people, the passengers, had nothing to do with the conflict. But before, nobody heard our screaming from the tents. Nobody wanted to hear or listen or learn about our sufferings. Nobody heard those who were tortured in jails. Or even if they knew they don't want to do anything about it. So, we couldn't see other ways, and we just used it for a short time, just to ring the bell in this world.[1]

This quote illustrates the political horizons of the PFLP in particular and more generally the Palestinian left of the period, their desperation, their personal daring and their devotion to the cause. It also hints at their broader politics and strategies.

The genocide in Gaza has raised for millions of people the question of Palestinian liberation, what it might look like and how it might be achieved. Many activists have been studying the history of the Palestinian movement, and particularly the history of the Palestinian left. The work of figures such as Ghassan Kanafani of the PFLP have been republished in English.[2] Several left publications have run articles featuring histories of the PFLP.[3] The PFLP and their ilk can seem to offer a genuine alternative to the degraded and degrading politics of the Palestinian Authority.

---

1. Quoted in Irving 2012.
2. See Brehony and Hamdi 2024.
3. See for example Leopardi 2024 and Kilani 2024.

This article will assess both the promise and failures of the Palestinian left. Although focusing on the PFLP, it will briefly also consider the Democratic Front for the Liberation of Palestine (DFLP). It will demonstrate how these organisations, despite their rhetorical commitment to revolutionary socialist internationalism, were fundamentally informed by a combination of Stalinism, Maoism and Palestinian nationalism. Ultimately, these politics would limit their horizons and confirm their status as a "loyal opposition" in the increasingly compromised Palestine Liberation Organisation (PLO).

The period of the 1960s and then the 1980s are both important in such a context. Both decades were moments of transformation, radicalisation and, in the case of the 1980s, mass mobilisation in which the Palestinian left played a significant role. Thus, this article will explore the politics of this section of the Palestinian left from the 1960s to the Oslo Accords in the 1990s.[4]

Origins

After the devastation of the *Nakba* in 1948, the main centres of political organising among Palestinians were to be found in the diaspora. The class differences that existed in the pre-1948 Palestinian population also found expression in the diasporic Palestinians. The poorest sections of the Palestinian population had been scattered, desperate and immiserated in refugee camps across the region, while the middle and wealthy classes managed to establish themselves with relative comfort in cities, albeit a comfort circumscribed by anti-Palestinian discrimination.

The green shoots of organising began in the 1950s among young middle-class Palestinians. Many of the individuals who later became leaders of the PFLP were students at the American University in the Lebanese capital. Beirut was a melting pot of many different political organisations and currents.

> The easy-going Paris of the Near East, which permitted capitalism
> and feudalism as it permitted freedom of the press, a feverish,

---

4.   There is a longer history of leftist organising in Palestine. For the history of the
     Palestine Communist Party see Buderi 2010.

bustling city of banks and publishing houses, which at that time was a haven for countless political refugees and a hideout for Kim Philbies of every persuasion.[5]

The 1950s was a period of insurgent regional anti-colonial nationalist movements. Gamal Abdel Nasser came to power in Egypt and ignited hopes among young Palestinians that a powerful Arab front could challenge Israel. By the late 1960s, however, it became clear that Nasser was reluctant to confront Israel militarily. In response, groups of young urban Palestinians struck out and took new initiatives. The most significant of these was the Arab National Movement (ANM), established by Palestinian Christian medical students George Habash and Wadie Haddad. As their name indicates the ANM was focused, at least initially, on building up a radical Pan-Arab movement. Their motto was "Unity, Liberation and Revenge". They felt that Arab unity and independence from foreign rule was a precondition for waging a successful campaign against Israel. "The way to Tel Aviv is through Damascus, Baghdad, Amman and Cairo", argued Haddad.[6]

By the mid-1960s the ANM had begun to develop a more left-wing sensibility that was informed by frustration with what they saw as the weakness and corruption of the local nationalist regimes and a compromised and indolent Arab youth. Political leader of the PFLP Ghassan Kanafani wrote an essay in 1957 called which is emblematic. In it he suggests that three-quarters of the youth of Damascus waste all their time playing backgammon in the street cafés. This generation, he says "is represented by the young man who stifles his yawn in the cafes of Damascus, walks out into the street at midnight, looks in a bored way up to the sky and asks his companion who leans drunkenly on him: 'Why has Arab unity still not been achieved?'" Kanfani despises this attitude and makes a call to arms.[7]

The ANM also rejected the conservatism of the newly formed Palestine Liberation Organisation. The PLO was the brainchild of Nasser and designed to circumscribe a more independent Palestinian

---

5.   Wild 1975.
6.   Quoted in Greenstein 2014.
7.   Wild 1975.

liberation movement. It was formally adopted by the Arab League in Cairo in 1964 and was led by several "notable" and wealthy Palestinians such as Ahmad Shukeiri. The PLO was actively rejected by the ANM, which emphasised the mass involvement of Arabs in their own liberation. By this stage, the ANM was starting to tilt leftward and began to adopt the language of socialism.

In an interview in 1998 George Habash described how socialism had initially "not been on our agenda" because there was a hostility toward the Soviet Union due to its support for the partition of Palestine.[8] This was gilding the lily somewhat, given that the class position of Habash and his compatriots made them suspicious of socialist ideas in the 1950s. Later however, particularly after the Ba'ath party came to power in Syria, socialism was incorporated more into the ANM's rhetoric. Thus, the ANM's motto changed and became "Unity, Liberation, Socialism, and Recovering Palestine".

> The age in which the movement of Arab nationalism was separated from the progressive social revolution has ended... There is no longer a political national question standing separately and posing against a specific social question called "the workers' question" or "the peasants' question"; or "the question of social progress".[9]

Meanwhile, in the latter part of 1958 and early 1959 in the Gulf States, another section of the Palestinian diaspora formed Fatah. Fatah would come to be the major political force with whom the Fronts would compete and define their politics. Contrary to the ANM, Palestine was the focus of Fatah. Like the ANM however, they were increasingly frustrated with the Arab leaderships and the staid, inactive PLO. Instead, they aimed to mobilise Palestinians in armed struggle for their own liberation.

> The only way to regain the robbed homeland is an organized revolutionary movement, unaffiliated, a movement that flows

8.   Soueid 1998.
9.   Quoted in Greenstein 2013.

from the heart of the Palestinian people, that will spring from all the territories surrounding the occupied land simultaneously.[10]

At the same time however, Fatah took money from the Saudi regime and was quiet about many of the dictatorial practices of other Arab states.

1967

The defining moment of this period for all Palestinian factions was the 1967 war. The defeat of the Arab armies by Israel disrupted many of the political certainties that had informed the Palestinian struggle. It undermined Nasser's prestige and represented a major defeat for the traditional leaders of the PLO. More broadly it was also a huge blow to the notion that the Palestinians could rely on Arab armies to aid them in defeating Israel. The Syrian poet Nizar Qabbani expressed this kind of sentiment in a celebrated poem written in the immediate aftermath of the war, "*Footnotes on the Book of the Naksa*":

> *Stirred By Oriental bombast,*
> *By Antarctic swaggering that never killed a fly,*
> *By the fiddle and the drum,*
> *We went to war and lost.*
> *Our shouting is louder than our actions,*
> *Our swords are taller than us,*
> *This is our tragedy.*
> *In short*
> *We wear the cape of civilization*
> *But our souls live in the stone age.*
> *You don't win a war*
> *With a reed and a flute.*
> *Our impatience cost us*
> *Fifty thousand new tents.*[11]

---

10. *Falastinuna (publication of the Fatah movement), 11 November 1960,* quoted in Baumgarten 2005.
11. Qabbani 1967.

The reference to the fifty thousand new tents was significant for the history of the Palestinian movement. The 1967 war had redrawn the lines on the map, created the Occupied Territories and vastly swelled the number of refugees living in the camps in Lebanon, Jordan and Syria. Conditions in these camps were desperate; hot, desolate, barren. Over time such populations would become restive and angry. Eventually this population would be a base for the fedayeen – the fighters of Fatah and the Fronts.

In 1968 Fatah fedayeen alongside the Jordanian military pushed back the Israeli military in the town of Karameh. A small piece of Palestinian territory was reclaimed. This moment seemed like a lightning bolt of hope, not just for Palestinians but regionally. It seemed to represent the possibility of a victorious guerrilla force against Israel. Hossam el-Hamalawy's history of the Egyptian left of the period describes the impact of the Battle of Karameh. He maintains that over 20,000 Egyptians volunteered to join the fedayeen and new leftist-led student societies spread in the Egyptian universities. "The Palestine cause was their main focus of propaganda and agitation."[12]

As a consequence of this action and an increase in regional funding, Fatah became the preeminent Palestinian organisation. According to the British Marxist historian Phil Marshall, it seemed to combine two deeply conflicted social forces, "Palestinian capital with the energies of the Palestinian masses: it seemed to reconcile the aspirations of the new bourgeoisie with those of the camps".[13]

Global turmoil

The PFLP's politics were shaped by more than merely regional politics. The late 1960s were aflame globally. The Algerians had kicked out the French. The Vietnamese were resisting American imperialism. Student rebellions were sweeping the US and Europe. In Latin America several guerrilla movements were also challenging for power. In China, the Maoist regime launched a hostile offensive against its internal enemies but badged it as a radical struggle of the youth. Millions of people across

---

12. el-Hamalawy 1977, p.65.
13. Marshall 1989, p.122.

the world turned to reading and political engagement. The Middle East was no different. George Habash describes how he developed his ideas:

> My Marxism grew deeper during my imprisonment in Syria. I am indebted to my jailer, Abd al-Karim al-Jundi, who kept me in solitary confinement for nine or ten months, thinking he would break me. I spent that entire period reading all the collected works of Marx and Engels, of Lenin, also of Ho Chi Minh and Mao.[14]

Sympathy and identification with the Maoist-influenced nationalist struggles of the day were not merely developed through abstract study. The influence of Maoism was literal, grounded in state-sponsored visits and meetings between Palestinians and the Chinese regime. In 1965 for example Kanafani visited China and met with the Chinese Foreign Minister Cheng Lee. According to Kanafani's wife, Anni Kanafani, he was "greatly influenced by the visit".[15] A year later in 1966 he attended the Afro-Asiatic Writers Conference. One story reveals much:

> A North Vietnamese writer after reading his speech distributed to the other members of the congress shrapnel souvenirs from the remains of an American plane which had been shot down a week before, Kanafani was so emotional that when his turn to speak came he choked up and couldn't read his prepared speech. Instead, he said he had nothing to offer in the way his North Vietnamese colleague had but promised to do so at the next conference. Then he sat down and burst into tears.[16]

The political tumult of this period found expression in the ANM and in late 1967 the PFLP was formed. George Habash described some of the political conclusions reached by the figures who would eventually lead the PFLP. It should be noted however that the "principle" of not depending on any regime or government proved to be very malleable.

---

14. Soueid 1998.
15. Kanafani 1973.
16. Wild 1975.

The war of 1967 and the new defeat brought a full revolution in our thought. We decided to adopt the Vietnamese model: A strong political party, complete mobilization of the people, the principle of not depending on any regime or government. The situation was now clear. The true revolutionary forces began to emerge. We are now preparing for twenty or more years of war against Israel and its backers. We have the moral determination and the guerrilla tactics to do so, and we will continue to do so, no matter how much Israel is backed by America.[17]

Class and the PFLP

The focus of the PFLP, as its name implies, was on Palestine and its liberation. According to the PFLP's founding documents, the primary enemy of Palestinians is Zionism and imperialism. Imperialism was defined as countries who were sympathetic to the US and Israel. Regimes that were not, were understood as progressive potential allies. These "progressive allies" included the Ba'athist regimes of Iraq and Syria.

The notion of the "popular front" was also key to the PFLP. The popular front was a policy developed by the Stalinist-dominated Comintern and then implemented by Communist parties across the world in the mid-1930s. It was an attempt by Stalin to strengthen the USSR's imperial position in the world and to develop an anti-German, Franco-British pact. Such an alliance necessitated the development of a less aggressive domestic posture among the Communist parties in countries that were aligned to the USSR. It therefore involved a directive to the international Communist movement to moderate their class hostility. Over time therefore the phrase "popular front" came to represent a leftist class-collaborationist approach to struggles.[18] In the PFLP's case the cross-class approach was given cover by revolutionary phraseology.

According to the PFLP the actors in the process of revolutionary national liberation were to be the "revolutionary masses". Palestinian resistance was the vanguard of the "Arab front", and the "Palestinian

---

17. Cooley 1973, p.139.
18. For more on the history of this term see Hallas 1985.

fighting masses on the occupied land are actors of the Arab revolutionary march against imperialism and its proxy forces".[19] There was an "organic link between the struggle of the Palestinian people and the struggle of the masses of the Arab people", as well as "the struggle of the forces of revolution and progress in the world".[20]

In its early years the PFLP drew heavily on Mao's theories to analyse Palestinian society. They identified three distinct classes: the proletariat (workers and peasants), the "petite" bourgeoisie, and the "haute" bourgeoisie. Following Mao, workers and peasants are the revolution's vanguard and primary beneficiaries. They are "[t]he material of the Palestinian revolution, its mainstay and its basic forces".[21] Members of this class form the destitute majority of Palestinians who "fill all camps, villages and poor urban districts".[22] The theoretical documents of the PFLP in this period maintained that the middle classes, or the petite bourgeoisie, should play a supportive role in the Palestinian revolution.

> Because the petite bourgeoisie's support for the revolution is not consistent, its members must be replaced by members of the proletariat in the leadership as soon as members of the proletariat are capable of taking over.[23]

In practice however, almost all the leading figures of the organisation were members of such a class; many had been doctors, teachers, writers or journalists.

For the PFLP the "haute bourgeoisie" was generally understood as an ally of imperialism, and therefore an enemy of the revolution. Nevertheless within it there were latent anti-Israeli sentiments which they thought could be aroused, at the appropriate time, to serve the revolution. The organisation was therefore riven with ambiguities toward the class forces, both Palestinian and regionally, for whom the Palestinian struggle was a vehicle to class or regional power.

---

19. *Popular Front for the Liberation of Palestine (PFLP)*, 1967 (Founding Statement).
20. PFLP 1969 (Strategy), pp.18–19.
21. PFLP 1969 (Strategy), p.47.
22. PFLP 1969 (Strategy), p.47.
23. Quoted in Cubert 1997.

Armed resistance

For the PFLP armed resistance was "the only effective method that must be used by the popular masses in dealing with the Zionist enemy and all of its interests and its presence".[24] The experiences of Vietnam, Cuba and China were the template. According to the PFLP's second convention these international battles involved "armed struggle to overcome the enemy's technological superiority through a protracted war commencing with guerrilla warfare and developing into a popular liberation war".[25]

The focus, at least in these years, on the armed struggle as the key strategy for victory was problematic in several ways. Firstly, the guerrilla struggle in Palestine was (and remains) in a vastly weaker military position to the overwhelming might of an Israel backed by the West. A strategy hinged mainly on armed struggle put the Palestinians on weak terrain. Furthermore, the Palestinian guerrillas had no strong and reliable military allies. The previous decades had shown how fickle the support for the struggle for Palestinian nationhood was from the larger military forces across the region. This capriciousness came not only from the "reactionary" regimes. The states with which the PFLP developed links, such as Syria and Iraq, provided limited and heavily conditional support for the struggle. They were concerned that support for the Palestinian struggle did not provoke revolt inside their own countries. According to Palestinian historian Rashid Khalidi, from the early 1970s in Syria,

> Assad and his fellow officers objected to uncontrolled Palestinian military activity dragging Syria into undesirable adventures. They opposed the freedom of action accorded to the heavily armed Palestinians within Syria. As regular military officers they desired a monopoly of weapons in Syrian politics.[26]

---

24. PFLP 1967 (Founding Statement).
25. PFLP 1969 (Strategy), p.72.
26. Khalidi 1984. Khalidi goes on to describe how during the Lebanese civil war the Syrian regime actively intervened with Israel to crush the Palestinian and leftist mobilisations.

Thus, the Palestinian factions limited their military activity in exchange for the right to continue to operate in Syrian territory. Such a quid quo pro ensured that the PFLP limited their political and strategic horizons. This was to their detriment. Regional, particularly working-class uprisings, including inside the so called "progressive" regimes, would have strengthened the hand of the Palestinians by weakening the networks of capitalist power across the region.

Archives have also revealed that the USSR was funding and facilitating certain activities of the PFLP.[27] The funding from the USSR and the Ba'athist regimes eventually had an influence over both the material and ideological contours of the PFLP's political outlook. Furthermore, as Australian socialist Mick Armstrong has noted:

> By tying themselves to these regimes, the PFLP downplayed the need to build a mass revolutionary movement from below throughout the Arab world. The PFLP ended up providing left cover for regimes like the Ba'ath in Iraq and Syria.[28]

Another problem with the emphasis on armed struggle was that the PFLP's rhetoric about the self-activity of workers and peasants was not matched in practice. The emphasis on armed struggle restricted the scope of popular mobilisation. Active participation in the actions and activities of the PFLP was often restricted to relatively few young men and left most of the rest of the population as supportive, often passionately supportive, but largely passive spectators. An oppressed population which sees itself as cheerleaders on the sidelines is both less capable of mobilising in thoroughgoing revolutionary struggle and ultimately incapable of creating a new society.

Finally, the focus on the guerrilla struggles helped popularise and entrench the dead-end politics of Maoism. A different political approach could have drawn on the industrial behemoth of the regional working class in a context of a period of intensifying class conflict.

---

27.   See KGB memorandum 1974, a message from Andropov to Brezhnev about the meeting between KGB station chief in Lebanon and Wadie Haddad, leader of the PFLP-EO (People's Liberation Front of Palestine – External Operations).

28.   Armstrong 2024.

Hossam el Hamalaway's thesis reveals how even by the late 1960s Egyptian youth, the poor and some workers were searching out political ideas and organisations.[29] An organisation which advanced a non-Stalinist, working-class politics may well have got a hearing and laid the basis for a party that could have intervened into the mass social rebellions of the decades to come.

The Democratic Front for the Liberation of Palestine

In the immediate years after the PFLP was formed there were two splits in the organisation. A right-wing faction headed by Ahmed Jabril broke away, declaring a desire to be "less ideological" and more militarily focused. He formed the PFLP (General Command). Another faction, headed by Nayef Hawatmeh, split to form what would become known as the Democratic Front for the Liberation of Palestine (DFLP). Historian Francesco Leopardi argues that:

> Hawatmeh and his comrades criticised the PFLP leadership for its authoritarian drift as well as for its excessive military caution. Moreover, the PFLP's left was composed of younger cadres who were closer to Maoist, but also Trotskyist, principles, giving to the dispute both a generational and an ideological dimension.[30]

The DFLP emphasised the need for a simultaneous "social and political revolution in all the Arab states, linked with the battle against Israel and with world imperialism led by the United States".[31] Therefore the DFLP initially placed significant emphasis on building relationships with non-military New Left organisations internationally, in particular with Israeli leftist anti-Zionist organisations such as Matzpen. Indeed Hawatmeh said in 2003: "We regarded Matzpen as a member of the common struggle in the problems of our two peoples".[32] They were also in touch with some Trotskyist organisations in Britain and elsewhere. In its early years, the DFLP emphasised the importance of social

---

29. el-Hamalawy 1977.
30. Leopardi 2020.
31. Democratic Front for the Liberation of Palestine (DFLP) 1975.
32. Matzpen 2003.

mobilisation as a vital feature of the struggle against Israel. They were also critical of the PFLP's relationships to the Iraqi and Syrian regimes.

The politics of Fatah and the Fronts were put to the test in 1970 in Jordan.

1970 and the aftermath of Black September

By the late 1960s nearly 70 percent of the population of Jordan was Palestinian. The country was ruled by the dictatorial Hashemite monarchy which was unable to control vast swathes of the country. Indeed, in many towns and villages the PLO was in charge. PLO forces ran the refugee camps, organised education and welfare, and were engaged in guerrilla training. The Fronts saw this positioning as allowing the Palestinians a base from which to launch a broader offensive against Israel. They called Amman the Arab Hanoi. The Fronts were also relatively clear-eyed about the Jordanian monarchy. They understood that the Jordanian rulers were not friends of the Palestinian masses and would prove an impediment to a generalised challenge to Israel (and therefore to imperialism across the region).

Therefore, from the late 1960s the Fronts had been calling for the overthrow of the Hashemite monarchy and for the PLO to take power. The leadership of Fatah was hostile to such declarations, fearing that overthrowing the monarchy would imperil the PLO's relationship with other regimes and wealthy backers across the region. The Fronts refused to curtail their activities and in September 1970 engaged in a series of plane hijackings and other attacks on Israeli infrastructure. Associated with this uptick in military offensives, the Fronts (working closely together) organised a "liberated zone" around Irbid, in northwest Jordan. This all proved to be the straw that broke the camel's back for the Jordanian monarchy, which launched a widespread military offensive against the PLO.

After hesitating for months Arafat began to understand that the Jordanian regime would crush all PLO forces that threatened their own power. Eventually, Fatah agreed to endorse a PLO call for a general strike and total mobilisation of the fedayeen. The call was issued on Sunday 13 September over Guerrilla Radio. The poor and disenfranchised of the camps, as well as the hundreds of thousands of Palestinian workers in the cities, heeded the call. Journalist John Cooley wrote:

> The guerrillas fought stubbornly, knocking out many Army vehicles with bazookas, the smaller RBJ rockets and heavy weapons fire. Teenage children of the refugee camps hurled grenades. Up in Irbid where the PDFLP had proclaimed a liberated zone and the "first Soviet of Jordan", al Fatah appointed Palestinian "military governors" with the approval of Arafat at the central committee. But food and water ran short; fires raged out of control; dead and dying lay in the streets while ambulances trying to reach them drew fire from both sides.[33]

While there was a significant response among the population, and the Fronts were correct in wanting to generalise the struggle, this moment of rebellion against a regional ruling class went down to defeat. The Iraqi and Syrian forces refused to enter the fight to back the PLO guerrillas and the regional working-class response was muted. In what became known as Black September, thousands of Palestinians were brutally murdered by the Jordanian regime, the centres of Fatah and Front organising were disrupted, and they were pushed out and forced to relocate, largely to Lebanon.

This period was the high point of the Fronts' radicalism. The story from here is one of compromise and political decline.

After Black September

In the wake of Black September, Fatah, still the dominant force in the PLO, drew the conclusion that to win a Palestinian state they needed to be more conciliatory toward the Arab ruling classes of the region. This trend was entrenched by the result of the 1973 Yom Kippur war, which saw a détente between the Arab regimes and Israel. In the aftermath the regimes felt they could engage with Israel on a more equal footing and began a process of dealing with Israel diplomatically. Thus began the long process of accommodation with Israel, which in turn had a

---

33. Cooley 1973, p.115.

conservatising impact on Fatah and therefore the politics of the whole PLO.

The DFLP, influenced by a "stages theory" of social revolution, was one of the first factions in the PLO to develop the idea of a Palestinian mini-state in the areas conquered by Israel in the 1967 war. They pitched this as liberated zones from which a further war would be waged. In this line they were encouraged by the Soviets, who were keen to settle down relations with sympathetic regimes in the Middle East.

In October 1974 the PLO was recognised by the Arab League as sole representative of the Palestinian people. Arafat spoke at the UN for the first time and the next few years saw a shifting of the goalposts from the demand for liberation of the whole homeland to an ever-decreasing area – "wherever could be liberated". This accorded very well with the interests of the Palestinian capitalist class – who were, by this stage, utterly dominant in Fatah. The DFLP, previously the most radical and leftward-moving section of the movement, backed the Fatah leadership. The PFLP, on the other hand, rejected the notion of establishing a Palestinian mini-state and formed "the Rejection Front".

The 1970s were dominated by a round of further war, radicalisation and then defeat in Lebanon, and eventually the centre of Palestinian organising shifted to the Occupied Territories in the West Bank and Gaza.

Intifada

By the early 1980s a generation of Palestinians were growing frustrated at the limitations on their lives caused by Israeli military occupation. Tensions were mounting and underneath the West Bank and Gaza there was, to quote the singer Ani Difranco, a fire just waiting for fuel. By the mid-1980s this resulted in an explosion of self-activity. Expansive networks began to provide the base for a reinvigorated Palestinian movement not based on fedayeen or militants, but rather the whole of civil society. This became a movement deeply rooted in the Palestinian masses.

In 1987, the killing of four Palestinian labourers by Israeli forces proved the spark that was to ignite six years of mass demonstrations, strikes, boycotts, stayaways, riots and the establishment of "no go" areas for Israeli troops. This would become known as the First Intifada or the Intifada of Stones. Journalist Joe Stork poetically described the symbolism of the stone throwing:

> The West Bank and Gaza is a land made in equal measure of stone and soil. The occupiers of the last twenty-one years have quarried the same stone to build their fortress suburbs that stand over this land. These constructions do not blend; they dominate. They are no more part of this landscape than the many tent encampments set up outside towns and large villages to garrison the tens of thousands of troops now needed to confront the stones. It is fitting that this uprising has reclaimed these stones to sling at the army, and to barricade the roads against their armoured vehicles.[34]

The emblematic figure of the Intifada was the young person hurling stones, head covered by a keffiyeh, standing defiant against heavily armed Israeli forces or tanks.

George Habash described the dynamic in the following way: "As for armed struggle, the PFLP advocated it until the Intifada. Under armed struggle, it is the fedayeen who fight, but under the Intifada, it is all the Palestinian people – children, women, artists, everybody".[35]

There was a radicalism to this movement and space for the left to grow. There was a deep hostility to collaborators with Israel and even, among some, animosity to the Fatah leadership of the PLO. One story here will suffice.

> The head collaborator of the camp, the mukhtar, had outlived many assassination attempts over the past several years. Recently, while he was away in Amman, some young men managed to break into his well-fortified home and in the bathroom they hung a portrait of Arafat with a noose. When he returned home

---

34. Stork 1989, p.67.
35. Soueid 1988.

and entered his bathroom, he had a heart attack and died on the spot.[36]

The Fronts in the Intifada

Over the early 1980s the Fronts had shifted their organisational focus to the West Bank and Gaza and increasingly began to intervene into different social sectors to recruit. The PFLP were implanted in the camps in Gaza, whereas the DFLP and the Communist Party both had influence in the West Bank. Although they were not big enough to fully rival Fatah, the left had built up enough support to be a significant element of the formal leadership of the Intifada. Problematically, however, the Fronts remained inside the structures of the PLO, committed to it, albeit with criticisms of the Fatah leadership.

While the early months of the Intifada were led by a combination of local spontaneous action and pre-existing formations, a more formal political leadership coalesced in early 1988. This became known as the Unified National Leadership of the Uprising (UNLU). Outside of the UNLU, and with growing influence, were the Islamist factions, Islamic Jihad and Hamas. The UNLU directed the course of the uprising through a series of communiqués. These communiqués, particularly in the early years of the uprising, would give each day of the week ahead a particular focus. The communiqués were assiduously followed.

> In the occupied West Bank people walk with their eyes lowered to the ground. This posture is not to avoid the attention of the incessant military patrols or to avert one's eyes from witnessing their physical violence. Neither do the downcast eyes indicate a population weary after twelve weeks of an uprising... Rather people look down to spot the latest statement from the Unified National Leadership of the Uprising, often found in the streets or tucked under a windshield wiper or door.[37]

In Gaza, the communiqués were broadcast outside radio stations to huge gatherings. The UNLU comprised both a political leadership on

---

36. Stork 1989, p.70.
37. Johnson, Lee and Hiltermann 1989, p.30.

the ground in the Occupied Territories and a diasporic leadership. The diasporic leadership's role was to develop the Intifada's strategic orientation. Over time a political cleavage developed between the leadership on the ground, in the midst of the uprising, and the external leadership.[38] The early articulated goals of the movement were to hold an international peace conference that could push for the establishment of a Palestinian state. This framework and these horizons were never seriously challenged by the Fronts.

As well as participating in the UNLU, the Fronts also established their own women's committees and student bodies. Importantly too, the trade unions became a field of activity.

The Intifada, Palestinian workers, the unions and the left

By the 1980s the Palestinian working class had become a more significant portion of the overall Palestinian population. The number of Palestinians working in low-wage jobs in both the West Bank and as day labourers inside Israel had increased. Unions grew. One union official estimated in 1985 that out of 150,000 workers in the West Bank, around 30,000 were union members. Women were also becoming wage labourers. Indeed, much of their increasing influence in political and social life emerged from their participation in trade union struggles.[39] Strikes were becoming an increasing factor in the struggle. Late December in 1987 saw a general strike of Palestinian workers across all the Occupied Territories. The strike extended to East Jerusalem – and was also universally observed by 650,000 Palestinians living inside Israel. Israeli profits in a variety of sectors, including hospitality, construction and fruit farming, collapsed.

By the time of the Intifada there were already several union federations and blocs, organised along political lines. The Palestinian trade union movement had, until the early 1980s, been dominated by the Communist Party (known as the Jordanian CP until the 1980s). The Communist Party had focused largely on bread-and-butter workers' issues, largely eschewing the national question. But the realities of Israeli occupation were bearing down on workers, and it was impossible

---

38. For more on this dynamic see Leopardi 2020.
39. Hiltermann 1991.

to separate the economic from the political; workers began to look to bodies that would address the question of the occupation. Although the CP maintained a significant presence the mood swung toward the factions inside the PLO, Fatah certainly, but also the Fronts. Both Fronts had made a turn toward emphasising working-class participation in the Intifada, declaring West Bank workers to be the vanguard.[40]

Although these struggles were vital, there were some significant limitations to the power of Palestinian workers. Israel was built to be an ethnically exclusivist state, with an economy that matched. A Hebrew labour policy was developed by the Israeli pioneers both before and after 1948 in order to limit the reliance of the state on Palestinian labour. In 1982, Jewish Palestinian Marxist Tony Cliff remembered his youthful years in Palestine. He describes the process of the establishment of Zionist separateness:

> The Zionists organised their own trade union, the Histadrut, which raised two political funds. One was called "the defence of Hebrew Labour", the other "the defence of Hebrew products". These funds were used to organise pickets to prevent Arabs working in Jewish enterprises and to stop Arab produce coming into Jewish markets. They did nothing to damage Zionist businesses.[41]

Over time such dynamics were consolidated. Although Palestinian workers dominated in some sectors, the core of the Israeli economy did not rely on Palestinian labour. This meant that, while Palestinian workers' strikes could be a crucial element in the overall struggle, they could not deal the knockout blow. Such a blow could only be achieved by regional working-class revolution. Nevertheless, Palestinian workers were very important for the Intifada. They helped give it a mass character and could point in the direction of what kind of forces were needed regionally to challenge both Israel and the dictatorial powers across the Middle East. In such a context the politics of worker mobilising became key.

---

40.   Marshall 1989, p.154.
41.   Cliff 1982.

The Fronts accepted the general line that the national struggle was paramount. This nationalist tendency of the unions led to a "freezing" of the class struggle inside Palestine and the creation of a "national alliance" between workers and the entrepreneurial class in the Occupied Territories. The words of one of the officials of the DFLP union body (the Workers' Union Bureau, WUB) spelled this out.

> The Israeli economic policy is aimed at weakening the Palestinian economy by putting restrictions and claiming taxes on Palestinian enterprises. So, workers have begun to compromise their own rights to protect the national industry, and therefore the national bourgeoisie. For instance, they gave up the thirteenth month pay. The WUB believes that there can to some extent be negotiations with the national bourgeoisie. There can be compromise, but not to the extent that everything will be loaded onto the workers' backs.[42]

So, the Fronts rightly saw that the workers' movement needed to have a political attitude to the occupation, but they wrongly subsumed themselves into the PLO. They made no distinction between themselves and the nationalists. Ultimately this meant that the Fronts refused to carve out an independent revolutionary working-class position. Although they maintained that the working class was vital, the Fronts did not argue that the workplace committees should play a leading role in shaping the political contours of the popular committees and their control over society. By the end of the first year of the Intifada there was a consensus that the popular committees were the basis for a Palestinian state. In such a context there may well have been room to argue that an expanded and deepened version of popular power – workers' power – was necessary. Even if such an argument was in a minority, it was the right argument to make. National independence, while important, does not bring genuine liberation for the nationally oppressed working classes. The history of post-colonial or post-independence states in the twentieth century has unfortunately not been

---

42.   Hiltermann 1991, p.77.

one where the newly independent state has become a paradise for workers. Far from it – as the examples of Egypt, South Africa, Iraq and Algeria demonstrate. So, Palestinian workers needed to fight for the struggle for national independence to become a struggle for socialism.

Workers' power in such a context should be the basis for a workers' state, not just an independent capitalist state. These arguments were deeply pertinent in 1987 and 1988 in the Occupied Territories.

Negotiations with Israel, nature of a Palestinian state, attitudes toward the Arab regimes

The other issues around which there was contestation and debate was what attitude to take to regional rebellions, the negotiations between the PLO and Israel and the USA and finally the nature and contours of a possible Palestinian state.

As the Intifada transformed from a brief uprising into a more sustained rebellion, there was more to fight for. The Intifada inspired regional uprisings from Algeria to Jordan to the Gulf States. These weren't rebellions just in solidarity with Palestine. They were rebellions that challenged the regional order. In Egypt mass demonstrations in universities were joined by workers from textile mills in Mahalla al-Kubra. Workers walked out and led a march in support of the Intifada while also raising slogans against the Egyptian dictator Hosni Mubarak. This was something the Fatah leadership could not countenance. So much of their existence and power was dependent on funding and support from these self-same regimes. They began to codify a policy of "non-interference" in the affairs of the Arab regimes.

Furthermore, the resilience of the popular movement was also considered potentially problematic by the Fatah leadership. While Fatah understood the popular committees as providing the infra-structure for a future Palestinian state, they did not approve of their radicalising dynamic. They wanted a movement that could be wheeled out and wheeled back in again according to the needs of its diplomatic negotiations. Fatah saw the mass movement only as a lever for its own power plays. Certainly, the Intifada had managed to change Israel's stance. The Israeli ruling class felt that they were unable to continue the occupation with the same structures in place. Similarly, the USA saw that it might well be advantageous to develop a Palestinian leadership that might be capable of containing an insurgent Palestinian movement. Thus, at the 19th Palestine National Committee meeting in Algiers in 1988 the PLO voted to declare a Palestinian state. Upon completing the reading of the declaration, Arafat, as PLO chairman, assumed the title of president of Palestine. This represented the absolute consolidation of Fatah's dominance in the PLO – a dominance which the Fronts did nothing serious to contest. In the wake of the agreement, Arafat toured the world to try and gain recognition for the new state of Palestine – as part of opening further negotiations with the US and Israel.

This process ultimately ended in the 1993 Oslo Accords and the establishment of the traitorous Palestinian Authority. The PLO voted to effectively recognise Israel as a legitimate state; and in doing so they trusted in the notion that the USA could act as a neutral arbiter in any negotiations with Israel. Fundamentally they propagated the disastrous notion that a Palestinian state could exist in peace next to an aggressive expansionist apartheid regime like Israel.

The Fronts were committed, to a greater or lesser degree, to the framework of international peace negotiations. As Leopardi argues:

> For its part, the PFLP had already gradually accepted the idea of an international peace conference in the years preceding the Intifada. After December 1987 however, the UNLU stated clearly among its goals the achievement of a settlement through the international peace conference. This became a systematic demand for the PFLP and in its positioning within the debate, it did not adopt a hard-line position. The PFLP stated several times throughout 1988 that both the landmark results scored by the uprising and the international détente allowed by the USSR-US rapprochement on several issues were paving the way towards the settlement of the conflict with Israel.[43]

Both the DFLP and the PFLP, in differing ways and at different paces,

---

43.   Leopardi 2020, p.180.

challenged elements of this trajectory while nevertheless maintaining their fundamental commitment to the PLO and its institutions. They oscillated wildly, denouncing Fatah one day but arguing to maintain loyal opposition to them the next. Hamas and Islamic Jihad on the other hand maintained a strident objection to the notion of a Palestinian mini-state and this objection stood them in good stead for the later betrayals.

At the same time, between 1991 and 1993 the Israeli arrest and killing campaigns eliminated many experienced leading activists. This repression occurred at precisely the same time as Fatah deliberately fragmented the movement. Arafat allocated PLO funds to institutions and personnel according to political loyalty, much to the detriment of genuine resistance activities. These two factors ultimately contributed to the decline of the mass character of the Intifada. Ultimately, the radicalism of the initial years of the First Intifada floundered. Israeli repression wore down the population, while the PLO pushed the struggle into more limited channels. The left had squandered opportunities to build a more serious, defiant opposition: one that looked not just to a deepening of the radical struggles of women, workers, students and camp dwellers but that also built more serious links with similar organisations in Egypt, Syria, Iraq, Lebanon and Jordan. Furthermore, there had been an opportunity to build a serious non-Stalinist revolutionary organisation to lay the basis for challenges to Fatah's leadership in the future. This was not done.

Conclusions

The more recent history of the Fronts echoes the story told here. It is a story of a loyal opposition that often offers reasonable critiques of the PLO leadership but fails to advance any serious strategies that might challenge it. In at least two instances, the revolutionary moments in Jordan in the late 1960s and in the first Intifada in the 1980s, there was the real possibility of a break with the prevailing politics of Fatah.

Israel and its Western backers are powerful. But so is the regional working class. Historically the Palestinian struggle has inspired those beyond the boundaries of Palestine. Political trends developed among Palestinians have been influential among broad layers of people, both across the region and the world. The failures of the Fronts are unfortunately the failures of the Stalinist and Maoist left of the period. The dead-end strategies of armed struggle, a misidentification of some Arab regimes as "progressive" and the subordination of working-class politics to the national struggle, are all tragic but recurring themes of the twentieth century. Their failures meant that increasing sections of the population became disillusioned with the left and looked to other political currents that claimed to be untainted, incorruptible and determined resistance fighters. In short, the failures of the left allowed the space for first Islamic Jihad, and then Hamas to grow.

The Palestinian struggle has been one of the most determined and brave in history. It has withstood phenomenal body blows and suffered greatly from Israeli brutality. Nevertheless, the history of the struggle cannot be merely understood as only shaped by Israeli and imperialist violence. The strategy and tactics of the resistance forces themselves must be assessed. The tragedy of the Palestinian left is that it has been unable to turn the "screams from the tents" into cries of victory. A revolutionary left needs to be built across the whole region. Palestinians are diasporic and have often formed the cadre of resistance movements regionally. What's more the Palestinian movement has proved to be the spark for many challenges to dictatorships across the world. In the West we must aim to build both solidarity and a revolutionary political movement that can aid such a project.

References

Armstrong, Mick, 2024, "The Terrible Legacy of Stalinism in the Middle East", *Red Flag*, 3 November. https://redflag.org.au/article/the-terrible-legacy-of-stalinism-in-the-middle-east

Baumgarten, Helga 2005, "The Three Faces/Phases of Palestinian Nationalism, 1948–2005", *Journal of Palestine Studies*, 34 (4), pp. 25–48.

Beinin, Joel and Zachary Lockman 1989, *Intifada: The Palestinian Uprising Against Israeli Occupation*, South End Press.

Buderi, Musa 2010, *The Palestine Communist Party 1919–1948. Arab and Jew in the Struggle for Internationalism*, Haymarket.

Brehony, Louis and Tahrir Hamdi (eds) 2024, *Ghassan Kanafani: Selected Political Writings*, Pluto Press.

Cliff, Tony 1982, "Roots of Israel's violence", *Socialist Worker*, 3 July. https://www.marxists.org/archive/cliff/works/1982/04/isrviol.htm.

Cooley, John K 1973, *Green March, Black September: The Story of the Palestinian Arabs*, Routledge.

Cubert, Harold 1997, *The PFLP's Changing Role in the Middle East*, Routledge.

Democratic Front for the Liberation of Palestine 1975, *The Political Program*. https://www.marxists.org/subject/israel-palestine/dflp/dflp-political-program.pdf

Greenstein, Ran 2013 "The Palestinian National Movement and the Anti-Colonial Struggle," Sociology Department University of the Witwatersrand. https://wiser.wits.ac.za/system/files/seminar/Greenstein2013.pdf

Greenstein, Ran 2014, *Zionism and its discontents: a century of radical dissent in Israel/Palestine*, Pluto.

el-Hamalawy, Hossam 1977, *"Uprising of Thieves" or an Aborted Revolution*, MA, American University in Cairo. https://arabawy.org/wp-content/uploads//2020/12/MA-Thesis-Hossam-el-Hamalawy.pdf

Hallas, Duncan 1985, *The Comintern*, Bookmarks.

Hiltermann, Joost 1991, *Behind the Intifada: Labor and Women's Movements in the Occupied Territories*, Princeton University Press.

Irving, Sarah 2012, *Leila Khaled: Icon of Palestinian Liberation*, Pluto Press.

Johnson, Penny, Lee O'Brien and Joost Hiltermann 1989, "The West Bank Rises Up", in Beinin and Lockman, *Intifada: The Palestinian Uprising Against Israeli Occupation*, South End Press, pp.29–42.

Khalidi, Rashid 1984, "The Assad Regime and the Palestinian Resistance", *Arab Studies Quarterly*, 6 (4), Fall, pp.259–66.

Kanafani, Anni 1973, *Ghassan Kanafani*, Palestinian Research Center, Beirut. https://www.marxists.org/subject/israel-palestine/pflp/kanafani-bio.pdf

KGB memorandum 1974, The Bukovsky Archive. https://bukovsky-archive.com/2016/07/01/23-april-1974-1071-aov/

Kilani, Ramsis 2024, "Strategies for liberation: old and new arguments in the Palestinian left", *International Socialism*, 183, Summer. https://isj.org.uk/strategies-for-liberation-old-and-new-arguments-in-the-palestinian-left/

Leopardi, Francesco Saverio 2020, *The Palestinian Left and its Decline: Loyal Opposition*, Palgrave Macmillan.

Leopardi, Franceso Saverio 2024, "The Left has Played a Key Role in the Palestinian Struggle", *Jacobin*, 7 February. https://jacobin.com/2024/07/palestine-left-pflp-habash-fatah-plo-hamas

Marshall, Phil 1989, *Intifada: Zionism, imperialism and Palestinian resistance*, Bookmarks.

Matzpen 2003, *Anti Zionist Israelis* (film with English subtitles, directed by Eran Torbiner). https://www.youtube.com/watch?v=upoACIfPIzs

Popular Front for the Liberation of Palestine, *Founding Statement and Platform of the Popular Front for the Liberation of Palestine*, 1967 and 1969. https://www.historyisaweapon.com/defcon1/pflp-founding.html

Popular Front for the Liberation of Palestine, 1969, *Strategy for the Liberation of Palestine*, https://foreignlanguages.press/wp-content/uploads/2020/08/S08-PFLP-Strategy-Lib-Palestine-7th-Printing.pdf

Qabbani, Nizar 1967, "Hawamish Fi Daftar al Naksa" (Footnotes to the Book of Defeat). https://allpoetry.com/poem/8526805-Verse-by-Nizar-Qabbani

Soueid, G 1998, "Taking Stock. An Interview with George Habash", *Journal of Palestine Studies*, 28 (1), Autumn, pp.86–101.

Stork, Joe 1989, "The Significance of Stones: Notes from the Seventh Month", in Beinin and Lockman, *Intifada: The Palestinian Uprising Against Israeli Occupation*, South End Press, pp.66–80.

Wild, Stefan 1975, *Ghassan Kanafani: The life of a Palestinian*, Mass Market Publishing.

EMMA NORTON[1]

Why socialists should oppose the sex industry

Emma Norton is a socialist activist in Sydney and a host of the Red Flag Radio podcast.

Introduction

Sex work is defended and even celebrated by many progressives today. This represents a significant departure from the traditions of the left. Historically, socialists and feminists saw the sex industry as a manifestation of women's oppression. Outlining the socialist position, Russian Marxist Alexandra Kollontai said in a speech in 1921: "Prostitution is above all a social phenomenon; it is closely connected to the needy position of woman and her economic dependence on man in marriage and the family. The roots of prostitution are in economics".[2] In addition, the industry depends on the sexist stereotypes and sexual objectification of women so prominent in capitalist society. The sex industry has a negative impact on society as a whole: it reinforces dehumanising attitudes towards women and other oppressed people, normalises male entitlement and preys on vulnerable women, perpetuating their disadvantage in the process.

Today, most of the left has abandoned this position. They glorify sex

1. Thanks to Louise O'Shea, who helped enormously in the early stages of writing, and to Jordan Humphreys, Diane Fieldes, Sandra Bloodworth and Grace Hill, who made helpful suggestions.
2. Kollontai 1977.

work as liberating and subversive or insist it is just another humdrum job, no better or worse than any other. Defending and even celebrating the sex industry has become a central part of progressive culture. It is common for left-wing people to take up the talking points and demands of sex industry bosses, celebrating such policies as unqualified wins for workers.

The shift towards a rosy view of the sex industry can be linked to the increased prominence of identity politics on the left. This involved moving away from more Marxist frameworks which viewed oppression as structural and social, towards a micro-level focus on individual identity, choice and personal preference. The rise of this individualist form of identity politics accompanied the neoliberal turn of the 1980s. The commodification of everything, including sex and bodies, was sold as liberating and empowering, as guaranteeing an individual's freedom to choose. Identity politics language suffuses the pro-sex work circles today. They defend sex work as individually liberating, a choice, a form of sexual expression and a sexual identity.

In opposition to this view, socialists should oppose the sex industry and view it as a symptom of the broader oppressions and inequalities of capitalism. This article will argue that commercialised sexual exploitation is incompatible with women's liberation and socialism. Socialists should fight for anti-sexist politics, and that includes staunch opposition to the sex industry.

Socialists aim to unite the working class to fight capitalism. Even the everyday struggle for reforms involves uniting ordinary people against capitalist institutions like the state. Socialists must be wary of bourgeois ideas which undermine class unity. Sexist ideas are particularly pernicious because they are subtly embedded in so many intimate interactions, and we are socialised to believe them from a very young age. The normalisation of the sex industry feeds into sexism, encouraging men to see women as sex objects who exist to satisfy the desires of men. This can only undermine working-class men's ability to see women as equals in the class struggle. When the left adopts a positive attitude towards sexual exploitation, we are undermining our own arguments against sexism and oppression and betraying that commitment to class unity.

Opposing a capitalist industry is not a foreign approach to socialists and the left. We oppose many industries considered destructive, divisive or oppressive. We argue to shut down the fossil-fuel industry, refugee detention centres, nuclear power plants and the weapons industry. This is not to morally condemn the people who work in these industries. Workers have little control over the structures of society and are not to blame for the existence of oppressive institutions. But the simple fact that these industries employ workers is no reason to defend them.

Our position on sex work cannot be guided by a knee-jerk reaction to the moralising of social conservatives and right-wing Christians. To the extent that they oppose the sex industry, they are not driven by concern about sexism and oppression, which they themselves perpetuate. While much of the Christian right are puritanical around sex, many other right-wingers believe that prostitution is a natural expression of male sexual appetites. Opposition to the right cannot be the political compass of socialists. We must objectively analyse the institutions of capitalism and understand their social role in order to arrive at a position consistent with our opposition to oppression and capitalism.

A note on language: throughout this article I will occasionally use the word "prostitution", both in quotes and my own formulations. The word has been mostly expunged from the writings of sex industry apologists, and my choice will be considered controversial. My aim is not to titillate or outrage. Rather, I believe that the widely adopted term "sex work" serves to sanitise a deeply exploitative and sexist phenomenon. I do not refer to people who sell sex as "prostitutes", because of the history of abuse and discrimination associated with that word.

The arguments of the sex industry apologists

Contemporary apologists for the sex industry dismiss concerns about sex work as a new form of prejudice, underpinned by a stuffy puritanical moralism that is anti-sex and hostile to individual self-expression. They tend to see sex work as a source of empowerment and liberation for women and queer people, the result of personal choice and sexual freedom.

An article in *Red Wedge* by a group of "pissed off sex workers" accuses "much of the left" of "clinging to the vestiges of a puritanical past".[3] They present the sex industry as a challenge to the traditional nuclear family and bourgeois sexual morality, thereby undermining a key pillar of capitalism. Some see "sex worker" as a sexual identity belonging in the LGBTQI+ rainbow, and champion sex workers as an inherently radical layer, responsible for many of the progressive movements of the past, including the sexual liberation movement of the 1970s.

Other sex industry advocates argue that sex work is no better or worse than any other job. The rallying cry of this crowd is "sex work is work". Molly Smith and Juno Mac, authors of *Revolting Prostitutes* who claim to have a "Marxist-feminist, labour-centred analysis", chastise those who focus on "sex as symbol" rather than the "'work' of sex work".[4] Smith and Mac demand that the left remain politically neutral towards the sex industry, seeing it as neither liberating nor oppressive. Our only tasks are to "destigmatise" sex work (to accept that it is no different from any other service industry), to fight for full decriminalisation, and to support sex workers' struggles for better wages and conditions.

Some manage to combine these two seemingly contradictory arguments, seeing sex work as both subversive and unexceptional. In a 2012 article in *Jacobin* magazine, Peter Frase wrote: "Not only does sex work destabilize the work ideology, it also conflicts with a bourgeois ideal of private, monogamous sexuality".[5] But Frase also firmly believes that "sex work is work". In the same article, he writes, "'Jobs' are degrading because capitalism is degrading, because waged work is degrading", thereby deflecting any criticism of the sex industry as *particularly* degrading and oppressive.

The pro-sex work arguments of the left are largely indistinguishable from the self-serving excuses of sex industry bosses. In Australia, Sexpo ("Australia's hottest adults only weekend") and the Sex Party (later the Reason Party, established by Fiona Patten, the former CEO of a sex industry bosses' association) have helped normalise and glamorise the sex industry. They argue that the sex industry is a site of female

3.   *Red Wedge* 2014.
4.   Smith and Mac 2018.
5.   Frase 2012.

empowerment, that it is a woman's choice to sell sex, that sex work is a job like any other, and only prudish "stigma" and legal restrictions make the industry unsafe.

To begin to understand the flaws with these pro-sex industry arguments, it is worth considering the relationship between sex work and consent.

Consent and economic coercion

> The global sex trade is built on the assertion that it is irrelevant whether the desire to have sex is mutual, as long as he pays, and she feels sufficiently compelled to accept the money. The money isn't coincidence; it's coercion. – Kat Banyard, *Pimp State*[6]

Most pro-industry advocates accept that sexual assault happens in sex work, but they do not see the whole transaction as inherently coercive and abusive.

Sex work involves *non-consensual sex* which has been economically coerced. The lack of consent from one party is overridden by the exchange of money, the primary method of coercion under capitalism. In other circumstances we would immediately recognise this scenario as morally and politically unacceptable: a teacher accepting sexual favours from a student in exchange for tutoring, charity workers accepting sex from refugees as payment for safe passage, bosses demanding sex from employees. There is an obvious power imbalance in each of these examples. A similar power imbalance exists between a sex buyer and a sex worker – one has the money which can provide a livelihood to the other. The sex between them is coerced. Of course, there is a qualitative distinction between rape and violence against sex workers and the overall coercive nature of the transaction. This is not an attempt to conflate violent attacks on sex workers with their everyday experience of sex work.

It is concerning that the modern, progressive understanding of consent is rarely applied to the circumstances that give rise to

---

6.   Banyard 2016.

prostitution. Consent is such a widespread concern that governments in countries like Australia are incorporating the concept into policy and legislation. The Commonwealth Consent Policy Framework explicitly states that consent is not "a problem to solve" or "a transaction or a contract – an exchange where someone 'gives' or 'receives' consent".[7] Economic coercion and the need to earn a livelihood are powerful factors which limit a person's ability to give free agreement to a sex act.

Many people who are sexually assaulted do not actively resist their rapists, for a variety of reasons. This obviously doesn't mean they are consenting to the assault. Just because the form of coercion is economic rather than physical, and just because sex workers consent to the coercion, we should not say that the sex itself is consensual.

The added problem for sex workers is that because a supposedly fair exchange has taken place, they often find it difficult to be treated as victims of sexual assault or coercion. As Rachel Moran puts it:

> That voice of shame that whispers in the ear of some abuse victims: "You can't say you were abused because you got enjoyment from it", is not dissimilar to the voice of blame that tells every prostitute: "You can't say you were abused because you got paid for it."[8]

While sex industry apologists often discuss the issue of assault in sex work, they usually argue that the way to prevent it is with regulations and the destigmatising of sex work. But even in a fully regulated and destigmatised industry, the same power imbalance exists, with sex workers submitting to the desires of sex buyers in exchange for money.

Pro-sex worker advocates often answer this argument about economic coercion by pointing out that *all* work is economically coerced under capitalism. This is true, and it is a big reason to be a socialist. It is also the case that most people believe sex is *different*, and that being coerced into sex is *worse* than being coerced into office work or truck driving. This is why progressives have argued for a new, broad understanding of sexual consent to be adopted by governments.

---

7. Australian Government (Department of Social Services) 2023.
8. Moran 2013.

Perhaps this view of sex *is* somewhat arbitrary and subjective. But why would the left want to challenge that? Would it be better to insist that sex, like every other aspect of our humanity, should be out of our control and exposed to the impersonal hand of the market? Besides, there is evidence that sex work is particularly psychologically traumatic, hinting at the importance of sexual autonomy for mental health. Kat Banyard cites a 2014 European Parliament report on sex workers in nine countries, which found that "68 per cent met the diagnostic criteria for post-traumatic stress disorder (PTSD) – comparable to the rate detected among survivors of state-sponsored torture".[9] Just because sex *can* be commodified and sold on the market doesn't mean it *should* be. Organs, wombs and even human beings are all sold on the market. The left should not sanitise such transactions by pointing to the fact that almost everything else is bought and sold on the market.

Responding to the apologists

Capitalism tends to normalise its worst crimes. Thanks to trite slogans like "sex work is work", sexual exploitation risks becoming completely normalised in modern culture. In opposition to these arguments, socialists must reclaim a position that clearly identifies the sex industry as a symptom of women's oppression and class inequality. The next section of this article will systematically combat the main arguments and myths touted by sex industry apologists.

Is sex work liberating?

Many apologists see the acceptance of sex work as the fruit of the sexual liberation movements of the 1970s.[10] But the hopes and dreams of those activists were quite different from the world we live in today. They saw sexual liberation as the emancipation of sex from all oppression, repression and coercion. Crucially, sexual liberation would free women from being the mere object of other people's desires. Consider John Berger's words in his 1972 BBC documentary *Ways of Seeing*:

A woman is always accompanied, except when quite alone, and

---

9.   Banyard 2016.
10.   See for example Gallant 2021.

perhaps even then, by her own image of herself... She has to survey everything she is and everything she does, because how she appears to others – and particularly how she appears to men – is of crucial importance for what is normally thought of as the success of her life.

This is how radicals in the 1970s understood sexism: as stultifying objectification which turns in on itself and defines how women move through the world. Berger's words are even more relevant today, when young women are encouraged to turn their entire lives into heavily curated online galleries, shaped by the opinions of anonymous followers.

Since the 1980s we have been sold an image of sexual liberation as *self-objectification*. Ariel Levy documented this phenomenon in her 2005 book, *Female Chauvinist Pigs*. Levy claims that women "traded the old, rigid model of femininity for a new, equally rigid one that says empowered equals sexualized". Women could stop playing the roles of demure virgin and Stepford wife but had to aspire to be "a caricature of a sex object", as Levy puts it.[11] They were encouraged to see sexual liberation in the latest clothing and makeup products, in pole-dancing and burlesque classes, and in going under the knife to meet ridiculous beauty standards. In lieu of any real liberation, women could now "choose" to revel in the commodification of their sexuality and the objectification of their bodies. Doing sexism to ourselves became the new feminism.

The glorification of sex work was part of this process. Glamorous autobiographies like *Diaries of a London Call Girl*, along with a slew of blockbuster films and TV, from *Pretty Woman* to *The Girlfriend Experience*, helped sell an image of prostitution as a viable career choice for the sexually liberated woman. Sex workers are portrayed as women in control, even dominating and controlling the men who pay them. Independent, high-class escorts became the glamorous new archetype of the modern sex worker, often portrayed as educated, well-paid

---

11.   Levy 2006 (first published 2005).

women who simply love sex, and whose clients pay for sophisticated, elegant company as much as sex.

The enlisting of women in their own objectification helped turn companies like Playboy into mainstream, respectable brands, and has made billions of dollars for the owners of tech platforms like OnlyFans and Instagram. But it should be clear that none of this was genuinely liberating for women. It merely encouraged women to obsessively cultivate a sexy and desirable image of themselves.

With the rise of the hustle-and-grind influencer culture of the past decade, many millions of people have found new ways to monetise sex and sexuality online. Symeon Brown documented this phenomenon in his 2022 book, *Get Rich or Lie Trying*. Brown points to the recent "renaissance in commercialised feminism". "At the heart of this movement", he says "is the questionable belief that anything that makes a woman rich is empowering for all women".[12] After Instagram, OnlyFans is the online platform which has profited the most from the online commercialisation of sex. Over 1.4 million content creators offer their content on OnlyFans, 78 percent of them are women and over 87 percent of their audience are men. The platform, which takes a 20 percent cut of all transactions, was started by Tim Stokely with loans from his investment banker father.[13] There is nothing progressive to be celebrated in social media empires making billions of dollars from the commodification of (mostly) women's bodies. Cardi B may promote the liberatory potential of online sex work because OnlyFans helped make her a millionaire, but most online sex workers do not make that kind of money. They are sold an elegant lifestyle and a quick path to riches, but usually find themselves having to sink countless hours and dollars into cultivating their image, from expensive cosmetic procedures to hours spent perfecting their photographs and feigning interest in an audience of voyeurs. As former sex worker Rae Story put it, "The internet sex industry has become the paragon of the idea of an idealised femininity as a sexual locality: a homing ground for masculine

---

12.   Brown 2022.
13.   Steven 2024.

gratification, distorted to look like female empowerment through exposure, manufacture and branding".[14]

Is sex work transgressive?

A common argument proffered by progressives in favour of the sex industry is that it challenges bourgeois sexual norms and the ideal of the nuclear family. Sex work itself is seen as transgressive, even as a radical challenge to capitalism. But this narrative misses the long history of prostitution as a *complement* to the institution of monogamous marriage. Since the beginning of class society, monogamous marriage and the control of wives' sexuality was a way for ruling classes to guarantee property inheritance through a restricted line of legitimate heirs. In pre-capitalist class societies like feudalism, prostitution was a relatively accepted way of upholding the sanctity of the marriage contract. The sexual servitude of a layer of poor women was a way to maintain the "purity" and virginity of upper-class women until marriage. In describing the European Middle Ages, Alexandra Kollontai said:

> The prostitute guaranteed that the daughters of the respectable citizens remained chaste and their wives faithful, since single men could...turn to the members of the guild for comfort. Prostitution was thus to the advantage of the worthy propertied citizens and was openly accepted by them.[15]

With the rise of capitalism, urban class inequalities drew ever greater numbers of women into prostitution. As Kollontai puts it, "The hypocritical morality of bourgeois society encourages prostitution by the structure of its exploitative economy, while at the same time mercilessly covering with contempt any girl or woman who is forced to take this path".[16] Despite this contempt, prostitution has never represented a serious threat to the institution of the family, even when it goes against the "morals" of the bourgeois family ideal. Capitalism has always been

---

14.   Story 2016.
15.   Kollontai 1977.
16.   Kollontai 1977.

able to straddle this seeming contradiction. It is the same contradiction inherent in the social construction of femininity under capitalism: the "whore" and the "virgin". Women are expected to satisfy the sexual and aesthetic desires of men, while also being respectable wives and mothers. Neither side of this unjust dichotomy is more subversive than the other.

An associated idea is that the experience of sex workers makes them an inherently subversive layer. Sex workers are seen as radical iconoclasts who refuse to fit society's restrictive sexual norms. Radical movements for social change are attributed to the influence and leadership of sex workers. In an article in *Xtra* magazine in 2021, Chanelle Gallant wrote that sex workers "have developed the most transformational sexual liberation politics of any social justice movement".[17] This view stems from an identity politics framework which assigns moral worthiness to people based on how downtrodden and marginalised they are. Gallant says it herself: the "diversity of marginalization" of sex workers is purportedly the reason they have "such an exceptional range of wisdom and analysis about systems of domination, how to stand up to them and how to survive".[18] In reality, being economically marginalised due to extreme discrimination does not turn people into radical anti-capitalists capable of combating the system. It just as easily forces them to focus on survival. Most sex workers are not in unions or engaged in political activism. They do not occupy a position of social power within the system, unlike workers employed in essential industries like healthcare. These *objective* considerations tell us far more about which sections of the population are the vanguard of the workers' movement and social change than the arbitrary moralism of identity politics.

Choice

Sex industry apologists argue that sex workers are merely exercising their right to choose what to do with their bodies. In this way they implicitly link sex work to other "rights to choose" that the left has championed for decades, such as abortion rights. Those who oppose

17.   Gallant 2021.
18.   Gallant 2021.

sexual exploitation are, according to this logic, denying women the right to choose, just like the conservative right and pro-lifers.

First, we should interrogate the concept of "choice" under capitalism. The catchcry of "choice" has been used by conservatives for the past forty years to promote the privatisation of social services, attacks on unions and the idea of personal rather than social responsibility. American right-to-work laws, also known as "workplace choice laws" have been enacted across 27 US states to weaken unions and lower wages. Similar language is used to dismantle government-run healthcare services in favour of for-profit providers on a private market. The grandfather of neoliberal thought, Milton Friedman, applied the same *laissez-faire*, pro-market attitude to the buying and selling of sex:

> You put a willing buyer [with] a willing seller, and it's up to them. You can argue with them that it's foolish, you can argue with them that it's a bad thing to do, but I don't see any justification for bringing the police into it.[19]

Friedman was no anti-police activist. He meant that the state and the public have no right to intervene in commercial activities of any kind, no matter how harmful. The left should be careful about taking up Friedman's logic. Just because someone chooses to sell or buy something doesn't mean that society has no responsibility or right to intervene in that exchange. We don't accept that opposing other industries unreasonably limits "the right to choose": weapons manufacturing, border patrol and the fossil fuel industries all rely on the labour of workers who "choose" to work in them, and the companies that "choose" to buy their services. This should not restrain our hostility to industries which destroy lives and the planet.

The big lie behind neoliberalism's favourite mantra is that we make "choices" in circumstances not of our own choosing, to paraphrase Marx. The reality is that most sex workers don't have many options. People do not choose to be poor, abused or homeless, but they can "choose" to try to escape that fate by selling sex. It's a "choice" that wealthy people

---

19.   From an interview with Friedman in *Chicago Life*, 2006. Quoted in Banyard 2016.

never have to make. Many people who become sex workers are driven by factors completely outside their control. A 2015 study of 250 indoor sex workers in the UK found that more than 70 percent had previously worked in healthcare, education or charities.[20] Government austerity has hit these sectors hard in recent decades and made working conditions tough. Some have seen sex work as a preferable choice to 13-hour shifts in nursing, or low-paid, highly exploitative work in child and aged care. Horrifying facts like these are often used by prostitution advocates to argue that sex work is no different from any other kind of care work. But that is a twisted interpretation. It is an outrage that decades of austerity and increasing wealth inequality have driven working-class women out of socially useful jobs and into prostitution. If the left's demands were met – to improve the social safety net and the wages and conditions of workers – fewer people would need to engage in sex work to survive.

The focus on personal choice is problematic in another way: it narrows our view to the psychology of individual sex workers and ignores the impact that the sex trade has on society as a whole. The industry perpetuates and feeds off some of capitalism's most misogynistic ideas about women: that they exist for the pleasure and satisfaction of others, regardless of their own desires. The normalisation of sex work, whether in brothels or online platforms, tells men that they have a right to purchase sexual access to women. And it tells women that their sexual desirability is a commodifiable asset to be bought and consumed by others. This is reason enough to oppose the sex industry, regardless of whether individual sex workers insist that they freely choose to sell sex.

"Sex work is work"

The phrase "sex work is work" is a truism. Sex work *is* work, by definition, but this platitude tells us nothing about whether we should defend or oppose the sex industry. Police work is work, guarding refugee detention centres is work, slavery is work. The word "work" does not

---

20. Taylor 2015.

absolve every horror of capitalism, a system capable of commercialising practically any aspect of human life and turning it into "work".

But even if we accept the "work" in "sex work", socialists do not treat all industries and jobs as equal. No industry has an automatic right to exist. Many are inhuman, destructive or the product of oppression. Unlike industries such as healthcare, prostitution cannot be repurposed and reorganised under workers' control to benefit humanity. Even though nursing is corrupted, undervalued and exploited under capitalism, it would continue to be essential work in a socialist society. We cannot say the same about prostitution, which must be abolished if we are serious about the goal of sexual liberation – ie for every individual to experience full sexual autonomy and freedom. This puts the sex industry in the same camp as other capitalist institutions that only serve an oppressive and destructive function, like the weapons industry or prisons.

While sex work may be work, there would be extremely problematic consequences if it was treated like any other working-class job.

In commercial activities, consumers have rights that are protected by the state. In the UK for example, consumer laws require that "the service be supplied with reasonable care and skill. In the event of a breach, the payer may be relieved of the obligation to pay, and may also sue for damages including loss of enjoyment, going beyond the price of the service itself".[21] If sex work was subject to consumer laws, courts could hear cases of clients suing sex workers for discrimination (eg when a sex worker refuses to have sex with a client due to some physical characteristic), for failing to deliver a service (eg when a sex worker changes their mind after payment), or for false advertising (eg if a sex worker advertises an extra service but then refuses to perform it).

If sex work was genuinely like any other job, it could be recommended by schools and universities to students. JobSeeker and other work-for-the-dole programs could force people to take jobs as sex workers or face a loss of benefits. People in other industries could be expected to perform sex work as part of their roles and have this stipulated in their contracts. The union movement has rightly fought

---

21.   Banyard 2016.

attempts to pressure women workers to carry out sexualised roles while at work, particularly in service industries where the objectification of women employees is commonplace. The historical position of the left was always to see such attempts as sexist attacks on workers' rights. The question remains: why should a major exception be made for the sex industry?

Even the most permissive legislation around the sex industry acknowledges that it is *not* like any other job, because it cannot be treated like any other job. After an uproar in Germany, the government ensured that work-for-the-dole programs could not refer dole recipients to work in brothels. This is because almost everyone instinctively understands that sex work *is* different from every other job, even when compared to the usual humiliations and suffering workers face under capitalism. Mass public opinion recognises that women shouldn't have to sell their bodies and sexual services to survive. Why would the left want to beat this progressive sentiment out of ordinary people?

The sex industry is also an occupational health and safety disaster. It breaks all the health and safety rules expected of other industries. If union standards were applied to the sex industry it would not be able to function. In every other industry, bodily fluids, such as semen, sweat and saliva, must be handled with extreme caution and effective barriers. No such protection is possible during prostitution, without wrapping the sex worker in plastic from head to toe. The usual standards of safety must be lowered to the floor for the sex industry to remain profitable. Safety conditions have been hard-won by centuries of union struggle. They are cherished and defended by workers in the best-unionised industries. On the Australian railways, workers regularly refuse to drive trains with potential safety defects, or to enter rooms suspected of containing asbestos and other hazards. Why should an exception be made so that pimps and brothel owners can make a profit? To do so undermines the position of all workers. Applying union standards of safety to the sex industry is utopian due to the nature of the work itself – which is to satisfy the sexual desires of buyers.

Sex work and the union movement

Advocates who believe that "sex work is work" argue that the trade union movement should defend the existence of the sex industry, embrace "sex worker unions" and advocate for decriminalisation. This position is a betrayal of the left's struggle to establish a commitment to anti-sexism in the workers' movement. That stance is not just a moral opposition to injustice, but an essential component of building class unity.

The workers' movement should be, in Lenin's words, the "tribune of the oppressed". Unions must not, in the supposed interests of a narrow section of the workforce, overlook the rights of oppressed people or of the working class as a whole. This is the classic error of economism, which has led union leaders and social democrats to take up reactionary positions on the basis that they appeal to a minority interest of the working class. For socialists, the key question is the class consciousness of the whole working class. The union movement should not support the sex industry because working-class consciousness should be avowedly anti sexist and against the sexual objectification of oppressed people. To endorse the idea that "sex work is work", or that the sex trade is an industry like any other, normalises sexist behaviour and attitudes that should be unacceptable in the union movement, which at its core seeks to unite working-class people to fight the bosses. That fight is undermined when workers accept divisive bourgeois ideas like sexism, or the idea that sex should be sold on the market.

Lenin's "tribune of the oppressed" idea is about the role of socialists in winning masses of workers to identify with *all* the oppressed and fight against *all* the injustices of capitalism. Only a working class with this socialist consciousness would be capable of overthrowing the system. Support for a sexually exploitative and sexist industry has a regressive effect on the social conscience of the working class. A socialist current within the union movement would fight to win workers to oppose the sex industry. Socialists don't accept workers' reactionary ideas about other issues. We want workers to understand the necessity of abolishing institutions like refugee detention centres or the police. The same should be true for opposing sexual exploitation and objectification.

The left of the union movement has always fought against sexism. Union members in the 1960s had to fight to rid union publications of sexualised caricatures of women. Office workers stood up against the sexist norm of managers conducting work meetings in strip clubs. Workers have opposed attempts to force women workers to go topless in bars, wear makeup and revealing clothing, or submit to sexual harassment. In recent years, when migrant workers on Australian farms were being coerced into sex with their employers, the United Workers' Union organised against such abuses.[22] A left which praises sexual objectification and exploitation is at odds with this anti-sexist tradition.

Unions must be intolerant of sexist behaviour by male workers and bosses, which can undermine the confidence of women workers and their capacity to fight back. Should women workers have to accept male workmates or fellow unionists paying women to have non-consensual sex with them? This is contrary to the task of promoting respectful attitudes towards women in the union movement. If we accept that such behaviour is perfectly normal and acceptable, what would be our argument against work meetings taking place in strip clubs? What leg would we have to stand on when opposing sexist bosses?

Socialists are not for excluding sex workers from the union movement or opposing their unionisation attempts. But so-called "sex worker unions" should not be uncritically supported. Sex workers, being some of the most marginalised people in society, are difficult to unionise. The prevalence of extreme poverty, precarious visa situations and controlling pimps in the sex industry means sex workers are unlikely to join official unions. Many "sex worker unions" end up including pimps, brothel managers and people whose main aim is to advocate for sex industry decriminalisation. This has been such an issue that some sex worker unions like the Scarlet Alliance have had to change their rules in response to criticism over the presence of brothel owners and managers in their ranks. The Scarlet Alliance now has a tiered membership structure: a first tier of sex-worker and ex-sex worker members, and a second tier which still includes non-sex worker "associate member organisations".

---

22.   Howe, Shi and Clibborn 2022.

Even so, it is difficult to distinguish the campaigns of sex worker unions from those of peak sex industry organisations. The Scarlet Alliance's main public campaign in recent years has unambiguously promoted the demands of sex industry bosses, opposing bans on strip clubs. A Scarlet Alliance press release last year rejected "the suggestion that strip clubs are responsible for gender inequality and disrespect of women [sic]".[23] Of course, it would be false to claim that strip clubs are *solely* responsible for gender inequality, but they certainly contribute to disrespectful and sexist attitudes towards women. The UK's Sex Workers Union (SWU) has campaigned numerous times against the closure of strip clubs and against zoning laws that exclude the sex industry. It should hardly be the role of the union movement to advocate for the rights of strip club owners to set up shop wherever they please. The union movement should not be insensitive to the rights of ordinary people, especially women, to not have a sexist trade in women's bodies in their community. We do not accept the right of other businesses to trade wherever they please. Attempts to construct power stations, highways and big shopping centres have faced public community pressure in the past due to their proximity to residential areas. Why should strip clubs and brothels be exempt from these considerations?

The main political role of sex worker unions and peer organisations has been to advocate for total decriminalisation, a demand also raised by sex industry bosses. This issue will be examined in full later in this article.

Stigma

> It isn't the stigma that kills people in the sex industry – it's the horrors of the job... You earn thousands and thousands of dollars each week, and it disappears on just surviving the life. – Simone Watson, former Australian sex worker.[24]

Often for pro-sex work campaigners, the *main* or *only* problem with the

23.   The Scarlet Alliance 2023.
24.   McCauley 2015.

sex industry is "stigma". Janelle Fawkes, chief executive of the Scarlet Alliance in 2015, claimed that: "Sex workers in Australia experience unacceptably high levels of stigma and discrimination and in some states criminalisation. Both public attitudes and policy approaches that harm sex workers are fuelled by those that refuse to acknowledge sex work as legitimate employment".[25] In other words, the main harm done to sex workers is due to stigma.

The sex industry does inherent harm to sex workers, and to society at large, quite apart from whether it is stigmatised. But before discussing this issue further, I want to thoroughly examine the realities of the industry that apologists want to "destigmatise".

The reality of the capitalist sex industry

The sex industry only thrives thanks to the injustices of modern capitalism: class inequality, and the systemic oppression of women, people of colour and LGBTI people.

The centrality of women's oppression to the sex industry

Most sex workers are women and girls. A 2014 report from the Urban Institute found that 78 percent of US sex worker respondents were cisgender females, 19 percent transgender women, and 3 percent male.[26] The extreme gender imbalance is an indication that the industry relies on the sexual objectification and oppression of women which is common to all class societies.

One factor in this is the overall wealth inequality that results from women's oppression. Women are more likely to find themselves in poverty and, as a consequence, be driven into prostitution.

Another crucial factor that drives the sex industry is the idea that women are sex objects, which can be internalised by women themselves. Girls and women are socialised by a sexist society and learn to think of and treat their bodies as objects of others' desires. A lap dancer interviewed by Natasha Walters for her book *Living Dolls* described the experience: "You just feel you can't make money any other way, that the most important thing about you is the fact that

25. Interview in McCauley 2015.
26. Brown 2014.

you are a sexual object, and that's what men want, and that's all you are".[27] Women and girls are taught to internalise the sexist attitudes of a society which constantly objectifies and undervalues them. When they find themselves in need of cash, is it any wonder that some women try to monetise that objectification?

While men are very unlikely to sell their bodies as sex workers, they are the overwhelming majority of sex buyers. This fact is worth reflecting on. We do not expect such a gendered consumer base in other service industries like aged care. Roughly equal numbers of women and men live in homes for the elderly. Men and women both grow old and require care. Similarly, men and women both have sex and experience sexual desire, so why are sex-buyers overwhelmingly men? The answer should be obvious: women are sexually objectified and oppressed in a way men are not, and men are taught to view women's bodies as objects they can purchase and control.

Extremely sexist attitudes surround the purchase of sex

It must be remembered, however, that only a minority of men purchase sex. A 2014 study found that around 17 percent of Australian men have bought sex at least once in their lives, and only 2 percent had done so in the past year.[28] The same study asked men who had stopped buying sex why they did so, with 72.3 percent saying: "I realized paying for sex is inconsistent with my morals". Men, even many who have bought sex, understand the immorality of using another person to satisfy one's own desires, without concern for reciprocity.

Why should a deeply sexist industry be "destigmatised"? Would society be improved if more men believed that women were sex objects who existed to satisfy their own sexual desires? We should be relieved to discover that, despite the sexist socialisation that men experience from a young age, only a minority think that paying for sex is acceptable. If we have stigma to thank for this, then stigma performs a useful social function by preventing more men from acting like sexist pigs. People who defend the sex industry are defending the rights of a deeply

---

27.   Walters 2010.
28.   Richters et al 2014.

misogynistic minority of men to economically coerce people into unwanted sex.

Class inequality

There is a tight correlation between poverty and sex work. Capitalism's extreme class inequality creates a section of the population who exist on the margins of the formal economy and must eke out a living selling their ability to labour and if not, their bodies and sexuality. The poorest sections of a country's population are overrepresented in the sex industry. Where poverty increases, prostitution tends to as well. When the 2008 economic crisis drove Greek unemployment up to 25 percent, the number of sex workers increased by 7 percent.[29]

Economic destitution drives prostitution. Thailand is thought to have the largest population of sex workers per capita in the world. It is also a country with high levels of poverty and unemployment among women, many of whom populate Thailand's sex trade. In Brazil, where 12 million impoverished people live in favelas (slums), there are estimated to be around 250,000 children in prostitution.

The class divide also drives the *demand* for prostitution. Sex buyers tend to be higher on the social pecking order than the sex workers whose services they purchase. While sex buyers exist across demographics of race and sexual orientation, a 2018 study found that high-frequency sex buyers are much more likely than other men to make US$100,000 or more annually.[30]

The labour supply of the sex industry is driven by poverty and marginalisation, while demand is often driven by the sense of entitlement of wealthy men to the bodies of poor and oppressed women.

Racism

Systemic oppression like racism and the oppression of trans and gay people, like women's oppression, contributes to people entering the sex industry. People of colour and LGBTI people disproportionately find themselves on the margins of the labour force, and therefore pushed

---

29.   Magra 2018.
30.   Demand Abolition 2018.

into the sex industry. They are also denigrated, demeaned and sexually objectified in ways that can be monetised.

Migrants make up a large proportion of sex worker populations in Western countries, if not the majority. This is because, in countries with higher standards of living and a social safety net, fewer citizens can be induced to work in the sex industry, whereas migrants denied the rights of citizenship are more likely to be induced to sell sex. In NSW, a 2012 study found that two-thirds of sex worker respondents were migrants and 46 percent rated their English language skills as fair to poor.[31] In Australia, most migrant sex workers are from Thailand, China or Korea. Migrants make up around 25 percent of the overall workforce in Australia, so they are overrepresented in the sex industry. Western Europe draws many of its sex workers from impoverished Eastern European and African countries. *Fondation Scelles* claimed in 2013 that two-thirds of France's sex workers were of foreign origin.[32] Poverty and the vulnerability imposed by visa conditions probably contribute to the overrepresentation of migrants in the sex industry.

The "supply" countries for sex worker migration and trafficking are mostly in Asia, Africa and Eastern Europe, where large numbers of poor and oppressed people form a potential pool of recruits into the global sex trade, through both violent and economic coercion. Eastern European countries devastated by war and economic collapse since the 1990s have become particularly notorious sites of sex trafficking. The industry for mail-order brides, which combines sexual exploitation with outright domestic slavery, follows the same routes, with women typically shipped out of Eastern Europe and Asia to marry men in the West. Many of these countries have also become destinations for sex tourism. Thailand is a notorious example, but Colombia, Brazil, the Philippines and Kenya are also popular spots for Western sex tourists. Racist stereotypes about sexually obliging non-Western women provide fuel for this horrific trade in human beings. US researcher Yasmina Katsulis cites the misogynistic and racist attitudes of sex buyers themselves. The administrator of one online sex tourism forum declared: "Women in Western countries are spoiled bitches… But there

31.   Donovan et al 2012.
32.   Goldmann 2013.

are many places in the world where women will treat you like a king for a minor fraction of what your Western girlfriend costs".[33]

Within Western countries, people from oppressed ethnic and racial backgrounds are overrepresented in the sex industry. An Urban Institute study found that 33 percent of US sex worker respondents identified as Black, though Black people make up 12.6 percent of the total US population.[34] Indigenous people are overrepresented among sex workers in New Zealand, Australia, Canada and the US. Higher rates of poverty and discrimination against these groups explain their overrepresentation in prostitution, but the industry also trades off stereotypes of non-white women as more sexually obliging. Katsulis found that in sex industry advertising, "Mexicanas are repeatedly portrayed as more open-minded and accepting, and a preference for the intrinsic asymmetry in the relationship is legitimized and naturalized".[35]

LGBTI people and sex work

LGBTI people are overrepresented among sex workers. Some progressives see this as a positive, and argue that "sex worker" is a marginalised sexual identity. Some have proposed adding SW to the LGBTQI+ rainbow. They also draw a particular connection between being pro-trans rights and pro-sex work.

The alliance between the LGBTI community and pro-sex industry groups has been corrosive. Many of the spaces of young LGBTI people are now suffused with a pro-sex work message. From Ru Paul's *Drag Race* to LGBTI activist campaigns, sex work is increasingly seen as a healthy and normal part of the queer experience.

The identity politics framework is more about *self-identity* than structural oppression. This framework depoliticises questions of oppression: identities are just seen as tastes and personal preferences, rather than historically oppressed identity groups. Sexual kinks and aspects of our personality are presented as identities, regardless of any connection to actual oppression. This is how sex workers and even sex

---

33. Cited in Banyard 2016.
34. Cited in Brown 2014.
35. Cited in Banyard 2016.

buyers are presented as a unique sexual identity. The left should reject this framework. Sex work represents the commercialisation of sexual activity, not a sexual identity. In fact, prostitution often involves sex workers having to repress their sexual identity and desires in order to satisfy someone else's. In her autobiography, *Call Me Sasha*, Geena Leigh describes how for decades as a sex worker she repressed her own sexual identity as a lesbian to service her male clients.[36]

With the depoliticised identity politics framework, nothing prevents us from seeing *sex buyers* as a sexual identity. Regularly paying for sex can be cast as an interesting kink, essential to one's identity. This demonstrates the absurdity of the identity politics framework. Buying people for your own sexual pleasure is not an identity, it is the expression of a power imbalance, of dehumanisation, and having internalised the idea that some people exist solely to satisfy one's own sexual desires.

Trans women are overrepresented in sex work. This is a symptom of oppression, of the extreme discrimination transgender people face in broader society. Transgender people are more likely to be impoverished, homeless, unemployed and suffer severe mental distress than cisgender people. In Australia, the unemployment rates for transgender men and women are double that of the general population. In addition, the high cost of gender-affirming surgeries and medications can be financially crippling. Derogatory stereotypes also contribute: LGBTI people, particularly trans women, are often treated like sexual curiosities who exist to satisfy the desires of others. These factors can drive LGBTI people into the sex industry for lack of better options. A telling 2017 survey of transgender people in Buenos Aires found that only 9 percent held formal employment, while 70 percent were sex workers, of whom 87 percent would leave the sex trade if offered formal employment.[37] Some of the key demands of the trans rights movement – for an end to discrimination in healthcare and employment – are not congruent with the promotion of the sex industry. If there was less discrimination, if transgender people were less marginalised, fewer transgender people would have to sell sex to survive.

36.   Leigh 2013.
37.   Cited in Valente 2021.

The socialist attitude to stigma

Given these realities of the sex industry, what should the socialist attitude be to its "stigmatisation"?

On the one hand, there is an unjustified stigma against sex workers. They often face discrimination in accessing services, police harassment and difficulty accessing employment outside the sex industry. This is because the authorities usually think of prostitution as the moral failing of individual sex workers, rather than a moral failing of capitalist society. This is the sort of hypocritical moralism that Lenin mocked in an article about the Fifth International Congress against Prostitution: "One lady from Canada waxed enthusiastic over the police and the supervision of 'fallen' women by policewomen, but as far as raising wages was concerned, she said that women workers did not deserve better pay".[38] This has been the general attitude of the authorities throughout capitalist history: to refuse to address the economic and social conditions that give rise to prostitution, while engaging in moralistic condemnation and policing of sex workers. Socialists should have no truck with this sort of stigma.

However, there is a justified stigma against the people who profit from prostitution and the men who pay for sex. This is part of a broader social rejection of sexual abuse and exploitation. In the last decade there has been a torrent of exposés of powerful men who have sexually assaulted and harassed women. There is, rightly, stigma and condemnation heaped on abusers like Harvey Weinstein. It is a continuation of this stigma to shame men who fly to Thailand for sex tourism trips, or who regularly visit brothels. Social shame is necessary in these cases, not because of the *sexual* nature of those activities, but because they are *sexist*, *abusive* and *exploitative*. Part of the hatred of far-right poster boy Andrew Tate is due to his unabashed involvement in sex trafficking and prostitution. Any attempt to "destigmatise" these outrageous behaviours only serves to normalise them and the misogyny which underpin them.

We also have some evidence of what "destigmatisation" looks like in practice. Germany's sex industry has been well-advertised

---

38. Lenin 1913b.

and publicly acceptable since its legalisation in 2002. Nisha Lilia Diu reported in the *Telegraph* that the German sex industry is "now worth 15 billion euros a year and embraces everything from 12-storey mega-brothels to outdoor sex boxes...known as 'verrichtungsboxen' – 'getting things done boxes'".[39] Since 2002, the number of sex workers in Germany has doubled to 400,000 people, servicing 1.2 million men per day. Destigmatising sex work has not in any appreciable way helped Germany's sex workers, who are now hyper-exploited in mega-brothels. But it has normalised the buying of sex, which is far more widespread in the German male population than in other countries. A 2022 study of 2,336 German men found that 26.9 percent had ever paid for sex.[40] Compare this extraordinarily high number to a Swedish survey which put the number of Swedish men who have ever purchased sex at 10 percent.[41]

"Stigma" is often presented as the singular cause of any and all harm to sex workers. This is blatantly false. The people who perpetrate the worst violence and abuse against sex workers are not random members of the public who think the sex trade is a disgrace, but the pimps and johns who approve of prostitution enough to benefit from it.

There is ample evidence that sex buyers are violent towards women. Regular sex-buyers hold more sexist, objectifying attitudes towards sex workers and women in general. Melissa Farley's 2015 study published in the *Journal of Interpersonal Violence* found that:

> Sex buyers were more likely than men who did not buy sex to report sexual aggression and likelihood to rape. Men who bought sex scored higher on measures of impersonal sex and hostile masculinity and had less empathy for prostituted women, viewing them as intrinsically different from other women.[42]

Sex buyers hold particularly appalling views of sex workers. The authors of a 2012 survey of 103 male sex buyers reported that:

---

39.   Diu 2013.
40.   Döring et al 2022.
41.   Public Health Agency of Sweden 2017.
42.   Farley et al 2015.

Twenty-five per cent told us that the very concept of raping a prostitute or call girl was "ridiculous". Nearly one-half of the buyers stated that rape happens because men get sexually carried away (47%) or their sex drive gets "out of control" (48%)".[43]

Given their atrocious attitudes towards women, it should come as no shock that regular sex buyers are more right-wing than the rest of the population. An analysis based on the statistics given by online escorts websites found that 55 percent of German sex buyers voted for the far-right *Alternative für Deutschland* (AfD) in the 2017 German elections.[44] It would in no way improve the position of women and other oppressed people if such misogynistic views and behaviours were "destigmatised", normalised and allowed to flourish.

Social shame and stigma are not inherent evils, they have been used by all human societies to discourage anti-social behaviour.

Disabilities and the "right to sex"

Another popular argument used to defend the sex industry is that every human being has a "right to sex" and, therefore, a right to purchase it. People with disabilities, it is argued, should have the right to purchase the services of sex workers, with government assistance if necessary.

This is one of the most emotionally manipulative arguments employed by the pro-sex work lobby. It is intended to recruit sympathies for disabled people to defend sexual exploitation. It is worth remembering that the majority of sex buyers are able-bodied men.

First, the "right to sex" can be a misleading phrase. Of course, everyone has a right to freely express their sexuality with other consenting adults, without interference from the state. But do people just have an automatic "right to sex" with someone who would otherwise be unwilling? This argument mirrors the sexist idea that men have insatiable sexual appetites that must be satisfied. Presumably, many rapists believe they have a "right to sex", as do right-wing "incels" who complain that women don't want to have sex with them. In reality, no one has a right to sex.

---

43. Farley et al 2009.
44. Arrow 2018.

Secondly, this argument is extremely patronising towards people with disabilities, branding them as inherently undesirable and only able to experience sexual intimacy by paying for it. Some people with disabilities, especially women, have baulked at this idea, and at the cynical use of their plight to defend a sexist and exploitative industry. In her article titled "Nobody's entitled to sex, including disabled people", Phillipa Willitts writes: "An infantilized view of disabled people also contributes to the idea that sex with one of us is *wrong* or *weird*, adding to the stigma and prejudice that limit our lives".[45] There are plenty of patronising limitations that capitalist society places on people with disabilities, including sexual ones. These are unacceptable, but the situation is not improved by allowing people with disabilities to participate in the sexual exploitation of other oppressed people.

Listen to sex workers?

Criticisms of the sex industry, like those outlined above, are often met with accusations of not "listening to sex workers". But there are problems with an understanding of the sex industry based purely on the testimony of sex workers.

First, there is a broad spectrum of opinion among sex workers and ex-sex workers. Accounts by former sex workers range from the glamorous to the harrowing, from Brooke Magnanti's *Diaries of a London Call Girl* to Rachel Moran's *Paid For*. There has been a tendency to dismiss critical accounts like Moran's and inflate titillating accounts like Magnanti's, which was made into a multi-season television show starring Billie Piper. How can the adage "listen to sex workers" be meaningful when their accounts vary wildly? Sex worker organisations similarly range in their opinions of the industry. There are pro-sex work groups which demand total decriminalisation and proclaim that "sex work is work". There are also organisations of ex-sex workers who call themselves survivors and demand the Swedish model which criminalises sex buyers. These testimonies alone cannot create a full picture of what the industry is, what it does to sex workers and its impacts on broader society.

45. Willitts 2014.

Secondly, most sex workers are not heard because they are some of the most marginalised and oppressed people in the world. Globally, a quarter are estimated to be children, and almost all sex workers belong to other oppressed groups: women, LGBTI and racially oppressed groups. The majority have no voice, no published books, no flashy screen adaptations. Very few active sex workers are members of sex worker organisations like the Scarlet Alliance in Australia. When we listen to such organisations, we tend to hear the voices of more middle-class, university-educated sex workers, people who no longer sell sex, or even people involved in pimping and exploiting sex workers. It has become common in such organisations to refer to the managers of escort agencies and brothels as sex workers. We must be careful, there-fore, that we do not end up hearing the voices of pimps when we try to listen to sex workers.

Thirdly, "listening to sex workers" doesn't tell us about the impact that the commercialisation of sex has on broader society. The sex trade is part of a broad swathe of social phenomena that encourage women to see their own bodies as monetisable commodities and men to see women as sex objects. As well as asking ourselves what sex workers experience, we must ask what the sex industry says about our society, and its impact on the consciousness of working-class people.

There are plenty of industries which are self-evidently bad for humanity. We do not need to first listen to the workers employed in these industries before forming an opinion of their damaging effects on society. Many workers in coal or weapons manufacturing believe the industries should continue indefinitely. But they represent a small minority of the overall working-class population. Similarly, even if some sex workers genuinely believe sex work is liberating and unoppressive, the left must take a hostile position to the sex industry. This is the only way to consistently oppose the oppression and objecti-fication of women and other groups.

Another problem with this logic is that, if we are to listen to the voices of sex workers, why not listen to the voices of sex buyers? In many other service industries, the left advocates for the rights and interests of consumers: from the treatment of medical patients, of elderly people in aged care, children in childcare and people with disabilities accessing support services. We care about people being overcharged, underserviced and mistreated in these industries. How could any of this apply to the sex industry, where "clients" purchase sex with otherwise unwilling partners? The language about privileging the voices of sex workers has no answer to this ambiguity.

The socialist position

A socialist position on the sex industry starts from recognising that prostitution depends on the twin capitalist injustices of class and women's oppression. It is the duty of socialists to expose and oppose all forms of oppression. To be consistent opponents of oppression we must oppose the sex trade. "Socialists" who mouth anti-sexist verbiage but think it acceptable for men to visit strip clubs and brothels are not worthy of the name. Tolerating this kind of sexist behaviour on the left says to women and other oppressed people: you are not equal comrades in the struggle, you are sex objects whose role is to satisfy the desires of others.

Ultimately, socialists are fighting for a society without class division or sexual oppression. In such a society, sex wouldn't be commodified or distorted by sexism, it would be liberated from all coercion. This is the meaning of the "sexual liberation" the left fought for in the 1960s and '70s.

As with most forms of oppression, sexual exploitation will continue so long as capitalism exists. As Lenin wrote, "no amount of moral indignation (hypocritical in 99 cases out of 100) about prostitution can do anything against this trade in female flesh; so long as wage-slavery exists, inevitably prostitution too will exist".[46] The only real solution is a long-term one: the overthrow of capitalism and its replacement with socialism.

In the meantime, it is important that socialists, the left and the union movement recognise prostitution for what it is – a deeply damaging symptom of an unequal, sexist society.

It is only from that vantage point, of principled opposition to sexism and exploitation, that we can formulate positions on concrete

---

46.   Lenin 1913a.

laws and policies, assessing whether they would be better or worse for sex workers and for the rest of society.

Is there a legal solution?

The debate between abolitionist feminists and sex industry apologists tends to focus on finding the perfect legal formula to either eradicate prostitution or to make it safe and "destigmatised". Socialists should be clear that no such formula exists – the capitalist state can neither end prostitution nor make it safe.

The left does not have some principled opposition to bans on destructive industries. There are many industries and trades which should be banned by the state: the left regularly calls to dismantle the nuclear weapons industry, and supports bans on child labour, slavery and organ-harvesting. The problem is that most outright bans on the sex industry harm the destitute people driven to sell sex, not the pimps who profit from it. This does not mean, however, that the left should flip into uncritically championing every bill which decriminalises a sexist and abusive industry. The call to "destigmatise sex work" too often means normalising the commodification of women's bodies.

The proposed legal regimes fall into four categories: full criminalisation, the Swedish model, legalisation and decriminalisation.

Full criminalisation, which makes it a crime to sell sex, buy sex, or profit from its sale, ends up targeting and criminalising the victims of sexual exploitation. In the US, where prostitution is criminalised in every state except Nevada, between 70,000 and 80,000 people are arrested in connection with prostitution each year, 90 percent of whom are prostitutes or pimps, 10 percent of whom are sex buyers.[47] Such laws only add to the over-policing of marginalised and oppressed communities. They leave sex workers at the mercy of police, pimps and johns. They also make it more difficult to leave the industry, because many sex workers acquire criminal records and serve jail time.

No feminist "abolitionist" today argues for the criminalisation of people who sell sex. They point instead to the Nordic Model, also known as the Swedish Model after the country where it was first implemented.

---

47. Farley et al 2009.

Such laws decriminalise sex work, while criminalising the *purchase* of sex, and claim to reduce *demand*. The Swedish government's taskforce in 2008 summed up the theory behind this law: "the primary factor that perpetuates both human trafficking and prostitution is demand, that is, that people, primarily men, purchase sex".[48] This is a truism: without demand the sex industry could not operate. But it conveniently sidesteps the various economic and cultural factors which drive "supply". The results of the ban in Sweden, Norway, France and elsewhere are hotly debated. Most of the evidence comes from studies with relatively small sample sizes, based on surveys of sex buyers and/or sex workers. It is still worth examining some of the evidence compiled over the past two decades.

The most compelling evidence that the criminalisation of sex buyers has protected sex workers in Sweden is that there have been no murders of sex workers by clients or pimps since the model was introduced in 1999, whereas client violence towards sex workers has continued unabated in decriminalised and legalised regimes such as exist in New Zealand and Germany. Surveys in Sweden, Norway and France show that the number of men buying sex has declined and that men see the laws as a deterrent.[49] In Sweden, the percentage of the male population who paid for sex fell from 13.6 percent in 1996 to 7.9 percent in 2008 and 7.4 percent in 2014, although more recent numbers are difficult to find.[50] Police departments report that Sweden and Norway have become undesirable destinations for sex traffickers since the bans were implemented, though there are no numbers to back up the claim. The Nordic Model also seems to have affected a change in public attitudes. By 2008, ten years after the model was introduced, 79 percent of women and 60 percent of men were in favour of banning the purchase of sex, compared to 45 percent and 20 percent respectively in 1996.[51]

The Swedish model has not abolished the sex industry. Trafficking continues, though it may have reduced. Some feminists have criticised

48. Swedish Institute 2010, p.5.
49. Kuosmanen 2011 and Fein 2019. See Coy, Pringle and Tyler 2016, p.2.
50. Coy, Pringle and Tyler 2016, p.4.
51. Both studies referenced in Cox 2021, p.44.

the Swedish government for providing too little funding to help people leave prostitution. Another downside is that the ban on the sale of sex relies on police enforcement. This may contribute to the over-policing of marginalised communities and of sex workers themselves. In terms of its overall effect, the Swedish Model has some benefits to recommend it. But, as with all legal solutions to a social problem, it relies on the repressive arm of the state to help solve an issue that is born of inequality, poverty and oppression.

Some sex industry apologists call for total legalisation, indeed – this is the logical conclusion of the argument that sex work is just another service industry. Legalisation existed for decades in Amsterdam and is currently in place in Germany. These regimes, in which the state props up and regulates the sex industry, have been a total disaster. They tend to normalise the abuses and, indeed, criminality, of the sex trade. A study by the London School of Economics in 2012 looked at trafficking in up to 150 different countries. It found that "on average, countries where prostitution is legal experience larger reported human trafficking inflows".[52] The legalisation of prostitution in Germany has turned the country into what *Der Spiegel* described as the "brothel of Europe". Widespread criminality and abuse continue there: the number of attempted murders of sex workers has increased since legalisation and trafficking flows have continued and increased in some areas. Despite legalisation, 90 percent of sex workers are unregistered and work without an employment contract. Organised crime syndicates continue to be heavily involved in the legal industry. Jürgen Rudloff was once the self-proclaimed "brothel king" of Germany, owning the Paradise chain of brothels. In 2019 he received a five-year sentence for aiding and abetting trafficking. Rudloff had been closely connected with the Hell's Angels gang who trafficked women into his brothels from Eastern Europe. In court, a former Hell's Angels gang member admitted to

> forcing women into prostitution at Paradise, setting them a daily
> target of €500 a day and beating them if they didn't bring enough

---

52. Neumayer 2013.

money home. He would hit them on the head, rather than the body, he explained, so that no one would see the bruises. He also tattooed his name on to women's bodies and ordered women to undergo breast enlargement surgery.[53]

This all occurred in *legal* mega-brothels throughout Germany, marketed as "male wellness centres".

Pro-sex work leftists usually acknowledge some of the problems with legalisation regimes like Germany's and instead call for the full decriminalisation of sex work. NSW, Victoria and New Zealand are held up as shining examples where decriminalisation has delivered on its promise to clean up the sex industry and protect the rights of sex workers. While decriminalisation is preferable to repressive laws which target sex workers, it has serious limitations. Client violence against sex workers has continued under these regimes, including brutal murders. A New Zealand government report found that "The majority of sex workers interviewed felt that the PRA [Prostitution Reform Act, which decriminalised prostitution] could do little about the violence that occurred".[54] Trafficking and organised crime involvement in prostitution have also continued.

The main problem with decriminalisation is that, like legalisation, it normalises the purchase of sex. This can negatively impact the way men view women and the way women view themselves.

The other problem is that "decriminalisation" often translates into *deregulation* of the sex industry, ie for the rights of brothel owners and pimps to ply their trade with fewer restrictions. In Victoria, the further "decriminalisation" of sex work in 2021 relaxed restrictions on sex industry advertising and allowed brothels to run without a license and sell alcohol. In New Zealand, health and safety inspections of brothels were found to be almost non-existent. The left never takes this sort of *laissez-faire* attitude to other businesses, which must be heavily regulated to defend the rights of workers, consumers and the broader community. Restaurants which prepare food are inspected to enforce safety conditions, bosses must be forced to respect workers' rights and

---

53. Lorenz 2019.
54. See New Zealand Ministry of Justice 2008.

zoning laws determine where businesses are allowed to operate. It is concerning that under the guise of decriminalisation, sex industry bosses are successfully deregulating brothels and escort agencies. Much of the push for decriminalisation involves opposing zoning laws which ban the sex industry from operating in certain locations, or from advertising widely. Again, this is an odd position for the left to take, and one we do not extend to any other industry. Destructive industries do not just have a right to operate where and when they please.

Proponents of sex work often assume that criminalisation and policing are the main source of criminality and violence in the sex industry. But the connection between the sex industry and organised crime has continued in countries where sex work is decriminalised or legalised. There are underlying reasons for the dominance of organised crime in the sex trade that are not reliant on the particular legal regime.

First, both sex buyers and sex workers often wish to remain anonymous. This leads to brothels and escort services keeping a low profile and many sex workers refusing to register, even in legal and decriminalised systems. The reality is that most men, even in the long-standing legal sex industry in the Netherlands, go to some effort to remain anonymous. This lends a clandestine nature to much of the sex industry that serves the need of organised crime to fly under the radar.

Second, sex industry bosses face hurdles in making their businesses profitable. The sex industry is "labour-intensive" and tends to have very low profit margins. Successful enterprises therefore exercise intense control over their workers and often look to trafficking as a source of cheap and easily controlled labour. Pimps tend to recruit and traffic sex workers who are extremely oppressed, tightly controlled, and paid very little. This is why coercion, abuse and illegal sex trafficking, facilitated by organised criminal gangs, are part and parcel of most sex industry business models, even where sex work is legal and legitimate.

Third, sex buyers, who are already willing to treat human beings like interchangeable sexual objects, tend to cultivate a taste for the degrading treatment of sex workers. This can include violence, rape, bestiality and sex with minors. The fact that such "appetites" are illegal in almost every country gives sex industry bosses ample reason to allow the criminal abuse of sex workers without reporting it to the police. Brothels, escort agencies and pimps who regularly reported such crimes would find their business drying up.

Fourth, many sex workers use drugs to help them dissociate from the experience of sex work. Drugs like alcohol, methamphetamine, cocaine and heroin are often used to self-medicate and shield sex workers from the psychological pain they endure at work. This need for dissociation drives many pimps to procure a steady supply of illegal drugs, another reason for the industry's association with organised crime.

None of these elements are dependent on the legal framework surrounding the sex industry.

The reality is that no laws under capitalism can end sexual exploitation or make prostitution safe. "Harm reduction" is a worthy and oft-touted goal, but it can be achieved by materially improving the lives of the women and marginalised groups most likely to be drawn into sex work. For example, increasing wages and employment options for women, Indigenous and LGBTI people, increasing welfare payments and access to childcare and healthcare, would all constitute real harm reduction.

Conclusion

Socialists must embrace a consistently anti-sexist approach to prostitution. Sex work is a symptom of a sexist and unequal society. It should not be raised on a pedestal as liberating or radical, nor should it be normalised through language like "sex work is work".

Identity politics and raunch culture have had a corrosive effect on left-wing politics. Identity politics has mangled the left's understanding of the sex industry in at least three ways.

First, because identity and experience are elevated above structural analyses of oppression, many have abandoned any understanding of women's oppression. Thanks to raunch culture, sexual objectification and other elements of women's oppression are ignored or even actively celebrated as a liberating choice. Some on the left have not only accepted sexist ideas around objectification but argue that to talk about "women" at all is transphobic, because it minimises the experience of trans women. "Woman" is certainly a social construct of our society. Transgender people, who transgress this socially constructed binary, are deeply oppressed and must be wholeheartedly supported by socialists. But the oppression of women is also a very real structural phenomenon, baked into how capitalism organises the family and work. It affects a majority of the world's population and is a key injustice of capitalism. The left must take women's oppression seriously and oppose it with gusto. That means recognising the sex industry for what it has always been: a symptom and product of women's oppression.

Second, individualism and neoliberal-inflected choice politics are elevated above the collective interest of working-class people. Sex work is seen through the prism of this individualism; as an identity category and personal choice rather than an element of structural oppression which has a negative impact on society and class consciousness.

Third, identity politics is intensely moralistic. This involves ranking the moral worthiness of groups based on how marginalised and stigmatised they are. This has led to the obsessive "platforming" of sex workers in progressive campaigns, particularly for LGBTI rights. Being pushed to the margins of society is a terrible symptom of oppression and discrimination. The marginalisation of certain groups is a social injustice to be fought. But it isn't edgy or radicalising, and it doesn't automatically bestow a liberatory consciousness on its victims.

There are sexist and anti-human assumptions at the core of the arguments put forward by defenders of the sex industry. They assume that prostitution is a natural part of life, that it has always existed and will always exist. Their most optimistic vision is for a world where women can freely choose to commodify their bodies without being shamed or repressed. This is a deeply regressive vision for humanity.

In its place we need a socialist vision, for a world without sexual exploitation or sexual oppression. In fighting for that world, the consciousness of ordinary working-class people matters. It is only by consistently opposing oppression that the workers' movement can unite the oppressed in a fight against capitalism. That means being clear about the inherently sexist and exploitative nature of the sex industry.

References

Arrow, Elly 2018, "*Compilation of Statistics on Sex Buyers in Germany*". https://ellyarrow.wordpress.com/2018/09/13/the-ultimate-compilation-of-statistics-on-sex-buyers-in-germany/

Australian Government (Department of Social Services) 2023, *The Commonwealth Consent Policy Framework*. https://www.dss.gov.au/sexual-consent/the-commonwealth-consent-policy-framework

Banyard, Kat 2016, *Pimp State*, Faber.

Brown, Elizabeth Nolan 2014, "*15 Facts About the Underground Sex Economy in America*", *Reason*, 14 March. https://reason.com/2014/03/14/economics-of-sex-work-in-american-cities/

Brown, Symeon 2022, *Get Rich or Lie Trying: Ambition and Deceit in the New Influencer Economy*, Atlantic Books.

Cox, K'reisa J 2021, *Vocation or Victimization: An Analysis of Legal Models*. Honors Project, Seattle Pacific University. https://digitalcommons.spu.edu/cgi/viewcontent.cgi?article=1142&context=honorsprojects

Coy, Maddy, Helen Pringle and Meagan Tyler 2016, "The Swedish Sex Purchase Law: evidence of its impact", *Nordic Model Information Network*, July. https://www.catwa.org.au/wp-content/uploads/2016/12/NMIN_briefing_on_Sweden_July_16.pdf

Demand Abolition 2018, Research Report: "Who Buys Sex? Understanding and Disrupting Illicit Market Demand", *November*. https://www.demandabolition.org/who-buys-sex/

Diu, Nisha Lilia 2014, "Welcome to Paradise. The effects of legalized prostitution in Germany", *The Telegraph, March*. https://s.telegraph.co.uk/graphics/projects/welcome-to-paradise

Donovan, Basil, Christine Harcourt, Sandra Egger, Lucy Watchirs Smith, Karen Schneider, Handan Wand, John M Kaldor, Marcus Y Chen, Christine K Fairley and Sepehr Tabrizi 2012, *The Sex Industry in New South Wales: a Report to the NSW Ministry of Health*, Kirby Institute, University of New South Wales. https://www.kirby.unsw.edu.au/sites/default/files/documents/SHP_NSW-Sex-Industry-Report-2012.pdf

Döring Nicola, Roberto Walter, Catherine H Mercer, Christian Wiessner, Silja Matthiesen and Peer Briken 2022, "Men Who Pay For Sex: Prevalence and Sexual Health", *Deutsches Ärzteblatt International* 119 (12): pp.201–207. doi:10.3238/arztebl.m2022.0107

Farley, Melissa, Jacqueline M Golding, Laura Jarrett, Neil M Malamuth and ES Matthews 2015, "Comparing Sex Buyers With Men Who Do Not Buy Sex: New Data on Prostitution and Trafficking", *Journal of Interpersonal Violence* 32 (23): pp.3601–625. https://doi.org/10.1177/0886260515600874

Farley, Melissa, Julie Bindel, and Jacqueline M Golding 2009, *Men Who Buy Sex: Who they buy and what they know, Eaves*. https://i1.cmsfiles.com/eaves/2012/04/MenWhoBuySex-89396b.pdf

Fein, Luba 2019, *"Has the Nordic Model worked? What does the research say?", Nordic Model Now!,* 22 December. https://nordicmodelnow.org/2019/12/22/has-the-nordic-model-worked-what-does-the-research-say/

Frase, Peter 2012, *"The Problem with (Sex) Work", Jacobin, 28 March.* https://jacobin.com/2012/03/the-problem-with-sex-work/

Gallant, Chanelle 2021, *"A revolution led by sex workers", Xtra,* 16 August. https://xtramagazine.com/power/decriminalize-sex-work-206843

Goldmann, Catherine 2013, *Current Assessment of the State of Prostitution,* Fondation Scelles. https://www.fondationscelles.org/pdf/current-assessment-of-the-state-of-prostitution-2013.pdf

Howe, Joanna, Elizabeth Shi and Stephen Clibborn 2022, "Fruit Picking in Fear: An Examination of Sexual Harassment on Australian Farms", *Melbourne University Law Review,* 45 (3): pp.1140–74.

Kollontai, Alexandra 1977 [1921], "Prostitution and ways of fighting it: Speech by Alexandra Kollontai to the third all-Russian conference of heads of the Regional Women's Departments, 1921", *Selected Writings of Alexandra Kollontai,* Allison & Busby. https://www.marxists.org/archive/kollonta/1921/prostitution.htm

Kuosmanen, Jari, 2011, "Attitudes and perceptions about legislation prohibiting the purchase of sexual services in Sweden", *European Journal of Social Work,* 14 (2), pp.247–63. https://doi.org/10.1080/13691451003744341

Leigh, Geena 2013, *Call Me Sasha: Secret Confessions Of An Australian Callgirl,* Allen & Unwin.

Lenin, Vladimir Ilyich 1913a, "Capitalism and Female Labour", *Pravda, 102, 27 April.* https://www.marxists.org/archive/lenin/works/1913/apr/27.htm

Lenin, Vladimir Ilyich 1913b, "Fifth International Congress Against Prostitution", *Rabochaya Pravda,* 1, 13 July. https://www.marxists.org/archive/lenin/works/1913/jul/26.htm

Levy, Ariel 2006, *Female Chauvinist Pigs: Women and the Rise of Raunch Culture,* Free Press.

Lorenz, Hilke 2019, *"Trouble in Paradise: the rise and fall of Germany's 'brothel king'"*, The Guardian, 22 June. https://www.theguardian.com/global-development/2019/jun/22/trouble-in-paradise-rise-and-fall-of-germany-brothel-king-jurgen-rudloff

Magra, Iliana 2018, "'They Don't Have Money': Greece's Prostitutes Hit Hard by Financial Crisis" *The New York Times*, 27 October. https://www.nytimes.com/2018/10/27/world/europe/prostitutes-greece-crisis.html

McCauley, Dana 2015, *"Pippa O'Sullivan, better known as escort Grace Bellavue, has died aged 28"*, news.com.au, 15 October. https://www.news.com.au/finance/business/other-industries/pippa-osullivan-better-known-as-escort-grace-bellavue-has-died-aged-28/news-story/9f8653462f0601199104069899365e83

Moran, Rachel 2013, *Paid For – My Journey Through Prostitution*, W.W. Norton & Company.

Neumayer, Eric 2013, *"There is a complex relationship between legalised prostitution and human trafficking"*, LSE, 15 January. https://blogs.lse.ac.uk/politicsandpolicy/legalised-prostitution-human-trafficking/

New Zealand Ministry of Justice (Prostitution Law Review Committee) 2008, *Report of the Prostitution Law Review Committee on the Operation of the Prostitution Reform Act 2003*.

Public Health Agency of Sweden 2019, "Sexual and reproductive health and rights in Sweden 2017 – Results from the population-based survey SRHR2017", 19 June. https://www.folkhalsomyndigheten.se/pubreader/pdfview/61789?browserprint=

Red Wedge 2014, *"Labor Intensive: In Defense of Sex Work"*, 23 August. https://www.redwedgemagazine.com/commentary/labor-intensive-in-defense-of-sex-work

Richters, Juliet, Richard O de Visser, Paul B Badcock, Anthony MA Smith, Chris Rissel, Judy M Simpson and Andrew E Grulich 2014, "Masturbation, paying for sex, and other sexual activities: the Second Australian Study of Health and Relationships", *Sexual Health*, 11, pp.461–71.

Smith, Molly and Juno Mac 2018, *Revolting Prostitutes: The Fight for Sex Workers' Rights*, Verso.

Steven, Khris 2024, *"40 Surprising OnlyFans Statistics to Know"*, Persuasion Nation, 15 August. https://persuasion-nation.com/onlyfans-statistics/

Story, Rae C 2016, *"The Middle Classing of Prostitution: The Social Climb of the Sex Industry"*, the f word, 3 April. https://thefword.org.uk/2016/04/middle-classing/

Swedish Institute 2010, "Selected extracts of the Swedish government report SOU 2010:49. The Ban against the Purchase of Sexual Services. An evaluation 1999–2008". http://www.xn--ntverketpris-gcb.se/DiverseTexter/TheBanAgainstThePurchaseOfSexualServices-AnEvaluation1999-2008.pdf

Taylor, Diane 2015. *"Most sex workers have had jobs in health, education or charities – survey", The Guardian,* 28 February. https://www.theguardian.com/society/2015/feb/27/most-sex-workers-jobs-health-education-charities-survey

The Scarlet Alliance 2023, *"Scarlet Alliance rejects call to ban new strip clubs".* https://scarletalliance.org.au/scarlet-alliance-rejects-call-to-ban-new-strip-clubs/

Valente, Marcela 2021, "Transgender job quota law seen 'changing lives' in Argentina", *Reuters*, 26 June. https://www.reuters.com/article/world/transgender-job-quota-law-seen-changing-lives-in-argentina-idUSKCN2E11QT/

Walters, Natasha 2010, *Living Dolls: The Return of Sexism,* Virago Press.

Willitts, Philippa 2014, "Nobody's entitled to sex, including disabled people", *Feminist Current*, 23 April. https://www.feministcurrent.com/2014/04/23/nobodys-entitled-to-sex-including-disabled-people/

JORDAN HUMPHREYS

Interview: A socialist view on the India-Pakistan conflict

Jordan Humphreys is an editor of *Marxist Left Review* and has written extensively on Indigenous oppression and working-class history. His book *Indigenous Liberation and Socialism is* available from Red Flag Books.

IN MAY 2025, Pakistan and India came to the brink of all-out war. Tensions escalated in the wake of the killing of 26 Indian tourists near Pahalgam, a town in Indian-occupied Kashmir. The Indian government accused Pakistan of sponsoring the attack and moved rapidly to expel Pakistani diplomats and suspend the Indus Water Treaty which gives Pakistan access to river water from Indian-controlled Kashmir. Border skirmishes between Indian and Pakistani troops then erupted in late April and early May. On 7 May the Indian government initiated Operation Sindoor, launching missiles at mosques in Pakistani-occupied Kashmir and directly into Pakistan itself, including near the city of Lahore. Thirty-one Pakistani civilians were killed in the strikes. The Pakistani military then launched its own missile strikes into northern India and Indian-occupied Kashmir. Sixteen civilians were killed and dozens wounded in what was the heaviest direct attacks between the two nations since the 1971 Indo-Pakistani War. On 10 May an uneasy ceasefire, brokered by the United States, was reached between the two countries. However, the underlying roots of the conflict remain.

The South Asia region is home to over 2 billion people, 25 percent of the world's population. Understanding the dynamics of this conflict then is important for socialists around the globe. In late May *Marxist Left Review* interviewed Imran Kamyana, a member of the national leadership of The Struggle, a Marxist group in Pakistan, about the background to the conflict and the debates that have emerged within the Pakistani and Indian left in response to its escalation.

Jordan Humphreys: *Let's start with the latest round of conflict in May. The Indian government said its military strikes were only a response to the killing of 26 tourists in Indian-controlled Kashmir, which it claimed the Pakistani military had some hand in. On the other side, Pakistan justified its military strikes against India on the basis that it was just defending itself against aggression. What is the truth behind all this?*

Imran Kamyana: First of all, from a Marxist point of view, the question of how a war starts, who started it, what the balance of power is between the different warring parties, is of secondary importance for us. Our starting point, as Lenin explained in his writings on the First World War, has to be the historical background of the war. Who is waging the war? What is the class character of the nations waging the war? Is this a conflict between an imperialist country and a colony? Or are these countries major imperialist powers or regional imperialist ones? For us the starting point has to be an analysis of what India and Pakistan are, the class character of these nations, and how they came into being in 1947.

Our organisation in Pakistan has a unique perspective on this question, which differs from the analysis of South Asia held by the Stalinist left.[1] We argue that Pakistan and India are both imperialist states. True, they may not be global imperialist powers on the scale of the United States, but they are regional or sub-imperialist powers. They both have imperialist designs in the region. Pakistan has imperialist ambitions in Balochistan, in Afghanistan and in Kashmir. The same goes for India, which is trying to exert more control over Kashmir,

---

1. This perspective is outlined in more detail by Lal Kahn, the historic leader of The Struggle, in Kahn 2003.

Nepal, Bhutan and Bangladesh. In recent years India has also been expanding its influence in Balochistan, which is occupied by Pakistan.

Both of these states then have this imperialist character and both occupy and plunder dozens of different oppressed nationalities in the territories they control. In Pakistan, there are three or four major separatist movements, some armed and some not.[2] In India, there are around a dozen such movements, including the Maoist insurgencies. Just the other day the leader of one of these insurgencies, the Communist Party of India (Maoist) was murdered by the Indian state.[3]

These two states then have an anti-working class, oppressive and imperialist character. In some ways, their position is similar to pre-1917 Russia. Tsarist Russia, while weaker than the Western European imperialist powers, had its own imperialist designs in Central Asia and Eastern Europe. Also like tsarist Russia, Pakistan and India didn't come into being through the classical fashion of the European bourgeois states that were established through revolutions.

In India and Pakistan, a new ruling class and capitalism were grafted onto this region of the world by British imperialism. When India and Pakistan emerged as independent nations in 1947 there was a basic continuity with the previous system established by the British. The new ruling classes of India and Pakistan continued the same brutal behaviour towards the working classes, the oppressed nationalities, the rural poor and women. They did this in different forms and in different guises, with new slogans, but their class character remained the same. What emerged after independence then was a comprador bourgeoisie in this part of the world. In India capitalism became larger and more powerful than in Pakistan, but the essential class character and capitalist nature of both nations is the same. In both countries, we have a capitalist ruling class that is dependent upon and complicit with imperialism.

Turning to the current situation. Why did India behave so

---

2. Oppressed nationalities in Pakistan include the Sindhis, the Balochs, the Pashtuns and the Saraikis, although there are other groups as well. The largest ethnic group is the politically dominant Punjabis.

3. Nambala Keshav Rao, general-secretary of the Communist Party of India (Maoist) and a leader of the Naxalite movement, was killed on 21 May by Indian security forces in Chhattisgarh.

aggressively? To start with, what happened in Pahalgam with the attack on the tourists is complicated. The Pakistani state has been carrying out a policy for many years of trying to manipulate the legitimate struggle of the Kashmir masses for the Pakistani military's purposes. They have sought to use Kashmiri groups as their proxies, and then India does the same in Balochistan and elsewhere. This is a very poisonous and very reactionary policy that the two states use against each other.

So what happened in Pahalgam? There was another incident which happened a few weeks before it. In Balochistan a whole train was hijacked by a separatist organisation, the Balochistan Liberation Army. They bombed the train and killed a lot of people, both civilians and soldiers. The Pakistani state blamed India for this, and India indeed has a history of supporting such groups both directly and indirectly. It is possible that Pakistan then supported the attack in Pahalgam as a retaliation for this attack on the train. But there are other possibilities too. Perhaps the Indian government knew it was coming and just let it happen. Or, and this is not impossible, the Indian government carried out the attack in Pahalgam more directly. In this part of the world, where we have a lot of covert actions and proxy military groups, things become very complicated as you can imagine.

At any rate, India escalated the situation with military strikes this time, but it is important to remember that in the past Pakistan has been the initial aggressor. For Modi, the motivation for taking an aggressive stand is related to his declining popularity. All the talk about India Shining is very exaggerated and that is becoming clearer to people.[4] There are also important elections coming up in Bihar, a major state, in November. In response to his declining popularity, Modi is inciting the flames of religious and communal hatred and divisions. And so you have this hyped-up anti-Pakistan rhetoric. In a way, it is similar to what Trump has been doing.

Then the Pahalgam incident happened and the hysteria ramped up. India launched strikes not only in Kashmir but directly into Pakistan itself, including near Lahore. From their point of view, it was impossible

---

4.   India Shining was a marketing slogan popularised by the BJP in the 2004 general elections in order to promote an image of economic optimism, both in India and to overseas investors.

for the Pakistani state not to respond and so they launched their own strikes against India. At this point, the Americans intervened to try and calm down the situation, which was rapidly getting out of control. Trump pressured both sides to accept a ceasefire. However, despite the fact that both India and Pakistan accepted this, India really has suffered a setback from these events. It acted very aggressively and talked big about taking on Pakistan and then backed down. In the aftermath, the Pakistani military has rebuilt a popular image among the masses and come out of this strengthened, while Modi comes across as weak and is attacked by the nationalist right in India for capitulating. He took a gamble and really he lost.

Jordan: *There are people on the international left or involved in the Palestine solidarity campaign who were very much on Pakistan's side in this conflict. They argued that Pakistan is resisting Western imperialism while India is on the West's side. Some even see Pakistan as like Palestine and India as Israel. What do you make of this argument?*

Imran: It is a typical campist argument. The whole idea is that the enemy of my enemy is my friend. It is a naive and stupid idea at best, reactionary and counter-revolutionary at worst. It is also notable that many who make this argument support Putin's invasion and occupation of Ukraine, despite claiming to be anti-imperialist.

Here in Pakistan, there is a section of the left who have this position. Some on the left argue that the Pakistani state isn't very good but under the circumstances, we have to put aside our criticisms and support it against India. For others, it also overlaps with the Muslim question. This is because Pakistan is the only Muslim-majority country with nuclear weapons, and so there is this idea that it is the ultimate protector of the Muslim world. Either way you end up just lining up with your oppressors, with the ruling class and the state.

We argue that in this conflict we cannot support either of these states; instead, we must advocate for an anti-war position that unites people from across the region against their governments. If open war did break out, we would of course try to safeguard the lives of people;

after all, we cannot welcome the enemy who won't be coming with flowers in their hands. They would rape, they would destroy, they would burn. But that doesn't mean supporting your own state or the military. The key thing is to fight to stop such a conflict from breaking out in the first place because if it did it would be absolutely devastating. Both the Indian and Pakistani governments have nuclear weapons and the official military policy is to use them if the integrity of either nation is threatened.

So sections of the left going along with one side or another in this conflict are just turning themselves into pawns for their own ruling classes and becoming minor players in this whole imperialist game.

Jordan: *India obviously has close ties to Western governments and to Israel which is partly why this comparison comes up, but I believe Pakistan also has a long history of collaboration with the United States. On the other hand, it also has a long-standing relationship with China. Has the growing rivalry between the US and China impacted Pakistan? Is this a factor in the current tensions between India and Pakistan?*

Imran: To answer this question we have to go back into the historical background. Pakistan and India both emerged out of the bloody partition of the subcontinent on a religious basis in 1947. The Soviet Union tried to forge ties with Pakistan after 1947 but the Pakistani elite rejected this and essentially became a part of the US camp in the Cold War. The Western powers supported Pakistan as a conservative religious buffer state against the spread of communism and Soviet influence in South Asia.

However, Pakistan balanced this support from the West with its relationship with China. Pakistan was the first Muslim country to recognise the People's Republic of China after the 1949 revolution. A lot of people think that the Pakistani state is stupid or naïve, but they are not dumb; in the pursuit of their own interests the Pakistani ruling class can be very clever and devious. Most of the time they know exactly what they are doing. They saw an alliance with China as important in containing the ambitions of the Indian government, which was allied with the Soviet Union. Pakistan supported China when it broke from the Soviets and then played a role in mediating between the US and China when Richard Nixon and Henry Kissinger started having meetings with Mao. After this Pakistan would go to China to get them to lean on the US to help them against India. And that's why the Pakistani military started getting all of this US military hardware, particularly the F-16 fighter jets, as well as Chinese weaponry.

In recent years, with the decline of US imperialism and the coming to power of clowns like Trump who are volatile and unpredictable, the situation has shifted again. It has pushed Pakistan to become closer and closer to China. It wasn't that they weren't close before, but with the West trying to use India against China, this pushes Pakistan into a closer alliance with China.

Until 1991 India was in the Soviet camp but after that India opened up their economy to Western capital. Before this the Indian economy had been very protectionist, a form of state capitalism was in place in which there was a lot of corruption in the ruling classes but also large amounts of state ownership and some state regulations and protections for workers. This ended with the collapse of the Soviet Union and the end of the Cold War. India then moved into the Western camp and established strong ties with the United States. The US hoped to use India as a counterweight to the growing military weight of China as it too grew out of the turn towards the world market. As tensions between the US and China grew, India became more important for the US and the West. This then reinforced China's relationship with Pakistan, you can see the imperialist logic of competition very clearly in all of this. Now China is giving more advanced weapons to Pakistan, there is even talk about Pakistan getting new generation fighter jets at discounted prices, which would be unprecedented. Chinese banks are indicating that they would help the Pakistani government to pay for these very expensive jets.

After the recent conflict, there has been a bit of a shift again. Pakistan has strengthened its position as a regional power. This will reinforce their ruthlessness inside and outside of Pakistan. Despite the US being close to India, Trump has surprisingly been quite positive about the Pakistani military. Both during and after the conflict he praised the Pakistani government as pragmatists with whom he could deal, and was cold towards Modi, effectively blaming him for the escalation. Perhaps it is because Trump likes tough military guys and rogue authoritarian states like Pakistan. He might think he can deal with them a lot more easily than more complicated nations like India. There are also trade issues between India and the US. Trump has forbidden Apple to establish new assembly facilities in India and attacked them over trade imbalances, whereas this isn't so much of an issue between Pakistan and the US.

However, Trump is unpredictable, so it isn't clear what this all means for the future relations between the US, Pakistan and India. But he did intervene quite strongly to bring the recent conflict to an end, and not on India's terms.

Jordan: It's interesting how much Trump is really impacting the whole world in different ways. Let's discuss the issue of Kashmir in some more detail. There is a long struggle for independence in Kashmir. However, as you said earlier there is also a history of both Pakistan and India intervening into Kashmir, and elsewhere in the region, in order to influence independence movements for their own purposes. What is your perspective on this issue? What should socialists say about the question of Kashmir?

Imran: In this part of the world the belated nature of capitalist development has created crisis-ridden and weakened capitalist states and a lackey comprador bourgeoisie. Capitalism has not been able to accomplish many of its historical tasks. In particular, it has struggled to form unified and stable nation-states. This is the case not just in South Asia but in other areas of the world, such as in parts of Africa.

This leads not to just one or two national questions but to dozens and dozens of national questions arising in response to the weakness of this belated capitalism. These nationalities were oppressed first by the British and then by the post-independence ruling classes when the new states of India and Pakistan came into being. These new states used the same policies of occupation, annexation, loot, plunder and oppression to try to crush these oppressed nationalities that threatened their new nation-states.

So having an answer to this complex situation is vital if we are going to build a revolutionary organisation in this region. To start with we endorse, without any hesitation, the right of self-determination for all the oppressed nationalities in this region. This includes the right of separation or secession for these nationalities. However, we don't limit ourselves to just supporting the right to self-determination. What we want to do is unite the peoples of the region into a voluntary socialist federation of South Asia – similar to what Lenin and Trotsky envisioned in the early years of the USSR before the Stalinist counter-revolution.

In terms of Kashmir specifically, this is a complex situation. Kashmir is divided by three different imperialist and regional imperialist powers. One part is occupied by Pakistan, another by India and yet another part by China. When the British left in 1947 they left a bloody wound in the body of South Asia and laid the basis for decades of violent conflict in this region.

We support the struggle in Kashmir for national emancipation against the occupation of these three countries. They should withdraw their forces and the Kashmiris should be given the right to decide for themselves, in a peaceful democratic manner, what form of state they want Kashmir to be. At the same time though, we oppose the imperialist powers, like Pakistan, manipulating this genuine struggle for national emancipation for their own ends. This happens not just in Kashmir but across the entire region, as I said earlier. The Kashmiris must be free to make their own decisions about the independence struggle without the intervention of foreign powers.

As well, while we support the struggle for independence, we discourage and criticise the strategy of the armed struggle. This question comes up not only in Kashmir but also in Balochistan, which is occupied by Pakistan. We oppose the armed struggle for a variety of reasons. To start with you cannot fight, and hope to win, against a gigantic imperialist power like India or Pakistan on the basis of the armed struggle of small militant groups. The armed struggle also discourages the involvement of the popular masses in political and class struggles. It also gives the bourgeois state excuses to violently oppress you even more, and this repression often extends beyond the militant groups themselves to all organisations or individuals involved in the independence movement, even those who don't support the armed struggle.

So this is our attitude not only to Kashmir but to the other oppressed nationalities in the region. We shouldn't water down our own revolutionary class-based program to appease nationalism, but we also shouldn't in any way take a position that aligns with our own oppressive imperialist state. We should present a socialist solution to the national question, one that argues that the way out of national oppression is through socialist revolution in the region.

We don't want to divide people, we don't want to erect new walls and new borders. Instead, we want to unite people – but on a free, democratic and voluntary basis. Lenin argued that even though Marxists support the rights of the oppressed nationalities, we also want to bring nationalities closer together and ultimately merge them in a future socialist society. So the Marxist perspective goes against the narrow nationalism and liberal nationalism that is influential among many of the oppressed nationalities in the region. But for this merging to take place we cannot support the oppression of the nationalities in any way, or condone imperialist states that occupy them against their will. So we believe that only socialism and revolutionary Marxism present a viable solution to the incredibly complex national question in the region. The only viable way forward for national freedom is working-class self-emancipation and socialism.

Jordan: To pivot to a different topic, would you be able to explain how the socialist left in India and Pakistan have responded to the current conflict? From what I have read, sections of the left in both countries have supported their own states, is this correct? In India, the Communist Party of India and the Communist Party of India (Marxist) have similarly taken a terrible stand supporting the Modi government's military strikes.[5] Is this a new problem for the left? And has there been a significant shift in positions on the left in the region in response to this current conflict?

Imran: This is not a new problem for the left in South Asia, but some sections of the left have gotten a lot worse. There have been three major wars between India and Pakistan as well as other minor conflicts, and much of the left took ambiguous or bad positions on these wars. However, for left-wing parties to openly support their own state's military action is unprecedented. In order to understand what has happened you need some background on the current state of the left in the region.

After the collapse of the Soviet Union the socialist left in Pakistan and India, as well as the workers' movement, retreated significantly.

This was much worse in Pakistan than in India, where the left has held on somewhat. In Pakistan, the vast majority of the socialist left disintegrated in the space of a few months after the end of the USSR. This idol that they had worshipped for decades was discredited and the Stalinist left just collapsed in response. Most of the members of the left-wing parties openly abandoned Communism. Some became born-again Muslims, others went into the imperialist NGOS and became moderate liberals. Again this happened in the space of only a few months, it was a very rapid shift to the right. That period was a very dark time.

Historically the largest group on the Pakistani left had been the Pakistani Peoples' Party. During the revolutionary movements of the 1960s, the Peoples' Party became a mass force in the struggle against the

---

5.   A 10 May press release states the Communist Party of India "believes that India had little choice but to respond firmly against the sources of such terrorism. The targeted nature of the strikes – avoiding Pakistani military assets and focusing solely on terrorist infrastructure – demonstrates a calibrated and non-escalatory approach, prioritizing accountability without inviting full-scale conflict. At the same time, CPI urges the Government of India to immediately call for an all-Party meeting to strengthen national consensus and collective resolve in the fight against terrorism". On 11 May the Communist Party of India (Marxist) stated in a press release that "there is a consensus across the political spectrum on the need to respond to the barbaric killings of Indian tourists in Pahalgam".

dictatorship. During this time a huge movement engulfed the country. Workers occupied factories, peasants took over the land, hundreds of thousands radicalised, and there was a revolutionary situation. Workers and peasants went well beyond demanding the end of the dictatorship and started raising openly socialist demands. The Stalinist left raised only democratic demands because of their two-stage theory of revolution. They lagged far behind the masses and so failed to make much headway. Instead, the People's Party dominated the movement.[6] The People's Party wasn't a revolutionary socialist party, it was a populist left-wing party. In 1971 the People's Party came to power, and once in office it began to shift to the right, making all sorts of concessions to the state and compromises with religious conservatives. Despite this, the People's Party government was overthrown by the military in 1977 and its leader, Zulfikar Ali Bhutto, was executed.

In the 1980s a small group of our comrades, mainly teachers, started to build a Trotskyist group. Before that, there had been a few attempts to build such a group but they had failed to work out. For a period in the 1990s and 2000s, our comrades formed a Marxist tendency within the Pakistan People's Party, but we abandoned this policy as the party moved to the right. It was very difficult to establish a group supporting revolutionary Marxism throughout this period, when the Stalinist left was collapsing and abandoning Communism and the People's Party was shifting in a more conservative direction as well. Despite this, our comrades laid the basis for a small organisation to emerge and grow into the future.

So in terms of the Pakistani left today and the debates over the war, the Stalinist left is much weaker than in the past, and while we aren't a huge party we are popular on the Pakistani left. And so our anti-war position, while not mainstream, has some influence on the left in Pakistan. Other sections of the left, and even some Stalinist groups, have adopted a relatively decent position because of this, not exactly the same as ours, but close, whereas those on the left who openly support the Pakistani military are not so dominant. There is also a section of younger left-wing figures in Pakistan who have studied at

6.   See Bell 2016 and Khan 2009 for an overview of the 1968–69 students' and workers' popular uprising in Pakistan.

elite Western universities and come back to the country presenting themselves as serious Marxist intellectuals in recent years. They have had a very conciliatory attitude towards the Pakistani state, essentially just asking that the state adopt their socialist policies. During this recent conflict, they supported the Pakistani military and were quite discredited on the left for this stance.

In India though the left is still dominated by sizeable Stalinist parties. There are four main communist parties for instance: the Communist Party of India, the Communist Party of India (Marxist), the Communist Party of India (Marxist-Leninist) and the banned Communist of Party India (Maoist), which is involved in the armed struggle.[7]

Historically these communist parties had the typical Stalinist two-stage theory of revolution. But with the passage of time, most have abandoned even pretending to have a second socialist stage at all. Now they believe that the communist movement should just fight for parliamentary democracy, for capitalism with a human face and for the secularisation of society. The failure of the left in India to present a pro-working-class program to the Indian masses is one of the reasons behind the rise of Modi.

So it was not entirely unexpected that the Indian left did not respond in a principled way to the conflict. However, the shameless and open support by the Communist Party of India and the Communist Party of India (Marxist) for the military strikes by the Modi government represents a new low for these parties. Of course, what happened in Pahalgam was a tragedy, but to say you stand with the Indian state in response is just a capitulation to Modi. The mainstream Indian left, in its current form, is in my opinion rotten to the core. This is the end result of its integration into the Indian state and its political degeneration. It is not surprising that they have lost a chunk of their popularity

---

7.   The Communist Party of India was founded in 1925. The Communist Party of India (Marxist) was founded in 1964 as a pro-China split, and quickly became the larger of the Communist parties in India. The Communist Party of India (Marxist-Leninist) was founded in 1969 as a split from Communist Party of India (Marxist), accusing them of adopting a parliamentary approach to socialism. The Communist Party of India (Maoist) was formed in 2004, uniting various pro-armed struggle splinter groups from the Communist Party of India (Marxist-Leninist).

in recent years because of this. There are smaller socialist organisations and individuals who have taken a principled stand against the Modi government and adopted a revolutionary anti-war position, but unfortunately, these are a minority on the Indian left.

Jordan: *What is the situation like in Pakistan after the ceasefire? A lot of the media are talking about the rising popularity of the Pakistani military and in particular General Asim Munir. What are the prospects for the left and the workers' movement going forward?*

Imran: As I mentioned earlier, the Pakistani state has come out strengthened from this conflict, at least for the time being. However, we should keep in mind that Pakistani capitalism is crisis-ridden. The economy is under an IMF program and they are tightening the noose around the Pakistani rulers and demanding more attacks on the working masses. The Pakistani state is trying to utilise its alleged victory over India to paper over this situation and strengthen itself politically, ideologically and militarily.

This is also important because the image of the military had been tarnished in recent years by the incarceration of former president Imran Khan and the crackdown on his supporters. Khan isn't a progressive figure, there are conservative and even far-right tendencies within his supporter base. They came into conflict with the state, but in Pakistan it is not at all unusual for right-wing forces to clash with the state. Often these very parties have been encouraged by the state at some point in the past, but then the state either crushes them or cuts them down to size when they gain too much independence. However, the crackdown on Khan did undermine support for the military for a period, whereas after the recent conflict, the state has been able to reassert its authority.

Pakistan has been in a deep crisis since 2007, which will continue to upset the legitimacy of the state among the oppressed nationalities and the working masses. The state will try as much as possible to utilise this alleged victory to promote an environment of nationalist hysteria in order to push back against this erosion of its legitimacy, but there are limits. They are still carrying out a ruthless neoliberal program of privatisation, increases to indirect taxes for the poor while cutting taxes for the rich, attacks on workers' rights and downsizing. Inflation and price rises are ruining the lives of ordinary people. There has been some resistance to these attacks, particularly by public sector workers. However, it is still too weak and scattered. The labour movement in Pakistan, like in many parts of the world, has been in decline for many decades. Despite this though, things can explode. In societies like Pakistan, the space for reforms is very limited and the state's authority can deteriorate rapidly, as we saw in Egypt in 2011 and in other explosive rebellions in recent years: Kenya, Bangladesh and Sri Lanka.

This applies not just to Pakistan but to India as well, which is a class-divided capitalist society. Indian capitalism is on the decline, not just economically but politically and even culturally. The nations in South Asia have been deformed by their historical development. They have arisen out of a complex amalgamation of feudalism and capitalism. From the past, we have all these religious prejudices that are mixed in with the modern achievements of science and technology, including the most advanced infrastructure. If you ever come to Pakistan you'll see first-class motorways as good as what exist in the Western countries, alongside extensive backwardness and illiteracy. This is the complex nature of uneven and combined development in this part of the world.

The recent conflict between India and Pakistan is another reminder that we need to build the revolutionary left internationally. It doesn't mean we should build in a hurry, or on a non-serious basis, but there is a real urgency to expanding the forces of the Marxist left. Socialism is not guaranteed, unlike what the vulgar Stalinist version of historical materialism once argued. When you look around the world today barbarism is more evident than socialism at this point in history. The genocide in Gaza is being live broadcast across the entire globe. You can see it on any news station, or you can go on the internet and watch it on YouTube and see what a genocide looks like. The threshold of tolerance for violence, bloodshed, oppression, and even open war has massively increased throughout the world.

But we know that only socialism offers a way out of this situation. So we should be more confident in Marxism. It is not some dogma, it is a scientific framework that explains the nature of the capitalist system and how to fight it. We should link all the issues that confront us – the climate crisis, the imperialist rivalries, the exploitation of workers, and the oppression of women and other groups – to the struggle for socialism. And every revolutionary must work out what role they can play in building the socialist movement and dedicating their life to that.

References

Bell, Jessica 2016, "The 1968–9 Pakistan Revolution: a students' and workers' popular uprising", *Marxist Left Review, 12, Winter.* https://marxistleftreview.org/articles/the-1968-9-pakistan-revolution-a-students-and-workers-popular-uprising/

Khan, Lal 2003, *Crisis of the Subcontinent, Partition: Can It Be Undone?,* Wellred Publications, London.

Khan, Lal 2009, *Pakistan's Other Story: The Revolution of 1968–69,* Wellred Publications, London.

LUKE HOCKING

What is liberalism?

Luke Hocking is a long-term socialist activist
based in Wollongong. He is a member of
Wollongong Against War and Nukes.

M ANY DIfFERENT PEOPLE with many different politics identify
with the tradition of liberalism. In Australia, the party of
right-wing conservatism is named the Liberal Party. On the
other hand, the radical student movement in the USA of the 1960s, and
many of the participants in the civil rights movement, were inspired
by liberal ideas. How can one set of ideas contain this wide breadth of
political positions?

Liberalism should not be seen as a set of values or ideas, as its
proponents suggest. Instead, it should be understood as a particular
class perspective. At its core, liberalism is the perspective of capital in
the abstract, derived from the framework of the commodity form. The
multitude of liberal traditions, and the inconsistencies within of each
of them, are no paradox, but are instead a reflection of the antagonism
between capitals, and of the contradictions inherent within the social
reality of the commodity form.

As with all political traditions, liberalism did not emerge or develop
in a vacuum but in concrete historical conditions. Economic and
social processes, most of all revolutions, have influenced liberalism

throughout its existence. The tradition has also had to come to terms with, and define itself against, rival political projects.

Despite its many forms and renovations, liberalism has never fundamentally escaped the problems of its birth. The liberal tradition remains trapped within its capitalist class basis, and for that reason can never solve its own internal contradictions, provide an accurate assessment of society, or act as a consistent guide to action for those who want a better world.

The material basis of liberalism

Liberals understand their own political framework as a series of ideas or values, often founded on the vague principle of "liberty". Usually, this includes the rights of individuals, standing for rationality, meritocracy and equality. By the mid-twentieth century, social progress and democracy were also, generally, included in the liberal grab-bag.

This is a vast simplification, though. Many different "liberals" disagree on which values are part of the tradition and which are not. Practically every thinker claiming the liberal mantle has attacked their political rivals for failing to include core tenets of the liberal canon.

The problem here is not that the liberal tradition cannot agree on which ideas are and are not liberal. It is the foundational premise of the debate that is the source of the problem. That is, liberals understand their own politics in idealist terms.

For a more serious understanding of liberalism, we should reject its own tools of inquiry, and instead turn to a materialist analysis. For Marxists, all ideas are rooted in the material reality of society, and especially the reality of class relations. Put simply, ideas have a class basis.

The class basis of Marxism is the working class. This is not to say that working-class individuals "invented" Marxism, or that workers will automatically take up Marxist ideas. But Marxism as a theory flows from an understanding of the position of the working class in capitalism, taken together with the lessons of the history of working-class struggle.

The perspective(s) of capital

Liberalism has a class basis too, though it is much more contradictory. In the most basic sense, liberalism is the perspective of capital. This only begs the question, though, because in reality capital can have many different perspectives based on its concrete situation. A more rigorous definition would be that liberalism is the perspective of *abstract* capital.

Unlike the working class, the capitalists are not a collective class. Their class interests can only be achieved individually, against both the workers they exploit but also against one another. That is to say, capitalist competition is the reason there cannot be one, true perspective of capital.

Liberalism, then, takes the perspective not of any specific capital, but of capital in general. To put it another way, liberalism as a political theory is not an attempt to theorise from the perspective of an actually existing capital, but is forced instead to try to understand the abstract perspective of abstract capital.

As a side note, the social layer that is best equipped to develop this theory is not a section of the capitalist class themselves. Their interests are too caught up in the day-to-day business of capital accumulation – trapped in the narrow, short-sighted perspective of their own profits. Instead, capitalism throughout its history has relied on a layer of bourgeois intellectuals to develop the theory and politics of the class as a whole. Liberalism is no less capitalist for having not come from the top-hat wearing industrialists themselves.

The commodity form

Liberalism's fundamental starting point, then, is a quite high-level abstraction – capital. It is possible to understand much about capital in the abstract from a historical generalisation; history proves time and again that capital seeks to expand, to revolutionise the means of production, to increase exploitation, etc. But a more solid theoretical foundation is required to properly explain liberalism.

Marx posits that the foundation of capital is the commodity: a thing with both a concrete use and an abstract (quantifiable) value, which is traded on the market.[1] Capitalism as a mode of production can be defined as the system of generalised commodity production. That is, when the logic of value, rather than anything else, is the prime determinant of society. This system requires, and culminates in, the commodification of human labour.

As a system made up entirely of social relations, this process is, of course, undertaken by human beings. Insofar as these individuals play a part in this process, though, they act not as human beings but as representatives of aspects of that social process. As Marx says in reference to the aristocratic landlord class:

> Every first born in the line of land owners is the inheritance, the property, of the inalienable landed property, which is the predestined substance of his will and activity. The subject is the thing and the predicate is the man. *The will becomes the property of the property* (my emphasis – LH).[2]

To follow the same logic, the capitalist is the embodiment of their capitalistic property. Theoretically, the standpoint of the capitalist is the standpoint of capital, which is itself the process of generalised commodity production under conditions of commodified labour. All this is to say that the social position of the capitalist is rooted in the commodity form.

The fundamentals of the commodity form accord with the core fundamentals of liberalism. Commodities confront the world as discrete units, which pass from the hands of one discrete owner into the hands of another discrete owner. The owner of a commodity, and especially the capitalist, thus similarly confronts the world as a discrete individual. In consequence, a framework that derives ultimately from the form of the commodity, via the perspective of the capitalist, will conceive of the world as made up of atomised individuals. The political individualism of liberalism reflects the social reality of individualism inherent in the commodity form.

The existence of the commodity form is also contingent upon

---

1.   Marx 1867, *Chapter I: Commodities, Section 1.*
2.   Marx 1843, *Part 5 (e): The Estates, "The state is the actuality of the ethical Idea".*

certain rights or freedoms of the owners of property. Centrally, the owner of a commodity must have the right to sell their commodity and buy others. Otherwise, the thing being exchanged is no commodity at all, but only a thing with a use, produced or acquired by extra-economic means (ie outside of a trade relationship).

Once again, this social dynamic leaves deep political imprints in liberalism. "Natural rights" or a rights-based framework are central to the liberal tradition. The foundational unit which "naturally" has those rights in the economic world, the commodity, corresponds to the foundational unit in the (bourgeois) social world, the individual. In a sense, individuals only have rights under capitalism as an extension of their capacity to own the real bearer of rights – commodities. As Pashukanis says:

> Having fallen into servile dependence upon economic relations surreptitiously created in the form of the laws of value, the economic subject – as if in compensation – receives a rare gift in his capacity as a legal subject: a legally presumed will, making him absolutely free and equal among other owners of commodities.[3]

Relatedly, formal equality, a central aspect of liberalism, is implied in generalised commodity production. On the market, there exists a certain reality of equality – everyone's money is worth the same. Any exceptions to this are, definitionally, extra-economic.

Commodified labour also creates a certain social reality of formal equality between human beings, by converting qualitatively different labour into quantifiable units of the same, interchangeable, labour power. Capitalism, that is, creates equality between people by considering them completely interchangeable. The way that this approach cannot help but ignore the reality of actually existing differences and inequalities (especially, but not limited to, economic inequalities) is reflected in liberal/bourgeois law.

Thus it is no accident that the bourgeoisie has "pitilessly torn asunder the motley feudal ties that bound man to his 'natural superiors',

---

3.   Pashukanis 1924, "*Introduction*".

and has left remaining no other nexus between man and man than naked self-interest, than callous 'cash payment'".[4] They are merely realising the implications inherent in the commodity form. Liberal equality has its roots in generalised commodity production.

It is worth noting that in material reality, the processes of capitalism never reach these "ideal" forms. "Perfect" capitalism has never existed and cannot exist, because of the contradictions of the process of capital accumulation.

This is a problem for capitalism (and thus for liberalism) but not for our purposes here. As we have established, liberalism is based not on actually existing capitalist reality but on an abstract, theoretical capital. This is why the commodity form, an abstraction predicated upon social relations, is so important. There is nothing else that can be the foundation of such an abstract philosophy.

Extra-economic compulsion and the commodity form

This can help us to understand one of the great conundrums of liberalism – the contradiction between freedom and force. This conundrum is indissoluble, as it is rooted not in a contradiction of ideas but in a contradiction of the commodity form itself. The social relation itself contains a paradox.

This paradox is relatively simple, if we consider how trade occurs socially. The owner of a commodity must be free to sell it (or not), but that freedom can only be guaranteed by force. It is explained most clearly by Colin Barker: "The exclusion of others from access to one's own property without one's consent is a necessary precondition of commodity-legal production, and material means are necessary to achieve this".[5]

It should be understood that this exclusion refers not just to the exclusion of non-property owners, but also to the exclusion of other property owners. In other words, capitalists have to protect their property from rival classes, but also from rival members of their own class. If one owner of property can seize the property of others, it undermines trade in general.

4.   Marx 1847, *Chapter I, "Bourgeois and Proletarians"*.
5.   Barker 2019, *"Violence and commodity producing societies"; "States and force"*.

The only way to guarantee the sanctity of trade in general, then, is to have some kind of force that acts not on behalf of a specific property owner, but of property owners in general. This force is the capitalist state.

The requirement for force to guarantee freedom (of property, particularly) explains how liberals can base their theories on the same premise and yet come to seemingly opposite conclusions. John Locke and Thomas Hobbes offer a good example. Both are foundational thinkers in the Enlightenment tradition that liberalism stems from.

John Locke, from the perspective of the individual right to property, arrives at a fundamentally libertarian philosophy. He argues that humans are naturally in

> a state of perfect freedom to order their actions, and dispose of their possessions and persons, as they think fit, within the bounds of the law of nature, without asking leave, or depending upon the will of any other man.[6]

Thomas Hobbes, on the other hand, justifies the greatest authoritarianism. So in *Leviathan*, he declares the need for an all-powerful absolute sovereign to prevent a condition where "there is no place for Industry; because the fruit thereof is uncertain"[7] – an opposite conclusion to Locke, yet predicated upon the same fundamentals: the right of the individual to freely dispose of their property.

Both thinkers are aware of the inverse of their own emphases. Hobbes suggests that "The right of nature...is the liberty each man hath to use his own power as he will himself for the preservation of his own nature".[8] And Locke demands "that all men may be restrained from invading others' rights, and from doing hurt to one another".[9]

Locke accepts, in other words, that were it not for the threat of a general force, the force of individuals (or, as Hobbes is also concerned

---

6. Locke 1690, *Chapter II, "Of the State of Nature"*.
7. Hobbes 1651, *Chapter XIII. "Of the naturall condition of mankind, as concerning their felicity, and misery: The Incommodites Of Such A War"*.
8. Hobbes 1651, *Chapter XIV, "Of the first and second naturall lawes, and of contracts: Right Of Nature What"*.
9. Locke 1690, *Chapter II, "Of the State of Nature"*.

about, the force of the masses) could disrupt the rights of property owners. No liberal since has been able to resolve the dilemma.

This is because the dilemma is a social one, and not something that can be overcome in mere thought. The commodity form, and therefore liberalism, is made up of a contradictory fusion of individual libertarianism and ruthless authoritarianism. There is no paradox here, other than the paradox of capital.

The historical development of liberalism

Liberalism, then, is rooted in the theoretical framework of abstract capital. This is a necessary starting point, but it is only a starting point. There are aspects to liberalism which cannot be fully illuminated by a process of logical reasoning alone.

This is because the political philosophy and practice of liberalism was not developed in the heads of thinkers who existed in a void, cut off from the world. Like all political traditions, it was developed in specific social and historical contexts. These contexts left their mark on the liberal tradition.

The roots of liberalism can be identified in the proto-bourgeois and bourgeois ideologies that historically preceded it. We have already mentioned the Enlightenment, which is the most important of these, but the line can be drawn back to the very beginning of the rise of capitalism in Europe.

The emergence of new capitalist productive relations was necessary for the development of capitalism. But capitalism's breakthrough from the margins of feudal society to become the dominant economic system required more than mere economic development. It required revolutionary social and political transformation – and this required ideas.

These ideas were developed as preludes to, as part of, and in the wake of social conflicts between the bourgeoisie and the feudal order. In this manner, new ideological reckonings became both possible and necessary for the rising bourgeois forces. Each conflict pushed the emerging bourgeois elements to make sense of themselves and their political and economic interests as a social layer.

In the womb of the old society

Economic development across Western Europe and Italy was such that by the fourteenth century there was already the basis for important pockets of capitalist relations of production, though commodity production was not yet generalised in any of these societies. Within the desert of feudal society, there were oases of proto-capitalism.

These oases generated the earliest proto-bourgeois ideas – articulated by John Ball and Wycliffe in England, and the thinkers of the Italian Renaissance. In Italy, the political forms of the city-states meant that, as Albert Weisbord puts it, "money-men...came into prominence. Entrenched behind the city-states under their control, they were able to develop a culture entirely their own".[10]

Renaissance thought was concerned mostly with the development of the arts and sciences. The fact that this early Renaissance emerged in Italy, within city-states that were dominated by semi-capitalist classes, meant that, at first, Renaissance thought did not concern itself much with politics and philosophy. But by the height of the Renaissance, with the forces of feudalism and the Church more openly resistant, a budding proto-liberal political philosophy was evident.

Machiavelli, who represented the culmination of Renaissance political philosophy, articulated support for a government which included the popular classes, and even for limited popular struggle against the aristocratic class: "in every republic there are two parties, that of the nobles and that of the people; and all the laws that are favourable to liberty result from the opposition of these parties to each other".[11]

Much to the disappointment of Machiavelli and his grand political and geopolitical vision (which can perhaps be summarised as authoritarianism in pursuit of liberty, foreshadowing Hobbes), the developing proto-capitalist economies of Italy were unable to be cohered into a state that was strong enough to support them against both the old order and their rivals elsewhere in Europe.

In Western Europe, the proto-capitalist pockets had provided the basis for a different trajectory. Chris Harman argues that though the

---

10. Weisbord 1937, *I, "The English Civil Wars"*.
11. Machiavelli 1513, *Chapter IV, "The disunion of the Senate and the people renders the republic of Rome powerful and free"*.

proto-bourgeoisie did not themselves challenge the feudal order in this part of the world, they did offer an "independent centre of power" which classes that *were* struggling against the feudal ruling class could look to, and which the feudal state could occasionally see an interest in developing.[12] The existence of these independent centres of power allowed the peasants' revolts of Western Europe in this period to push back against feudal forms of labour and thus increase the economic base of proto-capitalism.

Harman explains the dynamic that followed:

> Caught between the past and the future, the monarchical states facilitated the growth of capitalist forms of exploitation, but also became a drag upon them at key moments in history. Then bitter class struggles alone could determine whether society moved forwards or backwards. And these struggles involved bitter clashes between rival exploiting classes as well as between the exploiters and the exploited classes.[13]

Throughout this period, the economic and political centres of the emerging class forces were to be found in parts of Germany, the Netherlands, Normandy (in the north of France) and England.

Religion and revolution

It is no coincidence that these places are also, for the most part, where the Protestant Reformation found purchase. Religion, like any other idea, is not something that exists outside a social context. Religious ideas should instead be understood as generated by specific forces in society, and utilised for specific ends. During the European Middle Ages, this was relatively straightforward – the Catholic Church provided the ideological underpinning for the aristocratic ruling classes (and, of course, for themselves where they played the role of the exploiting landlord).

Even in this period, though, there were various "heretical" sects associated with peasant and/or urban discontent. Marxists should

12. Harman 1989, *"The class struggle and the transition"*.
13. Harman 1989, *"The class struggle and the transition"*.

understand these religious movements as attempts by oppressed and exploited social layers to develop or popularise ideas that justified their struggles. The fact that these ideas were understood in religious terms does not undermine this evaluation, as religion was the terrain of ideology at this point in time.

The Protestant Reformation of the sixteenth century was qualitatively different from the preceding "religious" conflicts, both in depth and breadth. The ideas of the Reformation represented the outlook of a growing layer of merchants and city-dwellers, who were restricted politically and economically by their landlords and the Church. The critiques that these layers developed could also mobilise the urban poor and the peasantry, who were being increasingly squeezed by the same forces.

Though Max Weber in *The Protestant Ethic and the Spirit of Capitalism* does not escape the bounds of idealism, he does provide a useful framework of what Protestantism actually stood for in its social context:

> Calvinism opposed organic social organization in the fiscal-monopolistic form... Its leaders were universally among the most passionate opponents of this type of politically privileged commercial, putting-out, and colonial capitalism. Over against it they placed the individualistic motives of rational legal acquisition by virtue of one's own ability and initiative. And...this attitude played a large and decisive part in the development of the industries which grew up in spite of and against the authority of the State.[14]

That this is a capitalist framework is fairly clear. But the hostility to "unfair" monopolies of the state is distinctly liberal. The Calvinists articulated an individualist creed, one that sought freedom (from extra-economic coercion) and equality (on the market).

Of course, not all Protestants were Calvinists, and not all Calvinists lined up neatly for the bourgeoisie. Different social forces came to

---

14. Weber 1905, *Chapter 5, "Asceticism and the Spirit of Capitalism"*.

oppose the general European order for different reasons, and the particular array of Protestant ideas that they adhered to reflected their social priorities. Despite these differences, though, the general framework of the Reformation provided the ideological foundation for the most important social conflicts of the era – the early bourgeois revolutions in the Netherlands and England.

In the Netherlands, as Pepijn Brandon argues:

> The Reformation formed the ideological background to the rising opposition movements of the 1560s. The relative openness of Dutch society, its urbanisation and its strategic position at a nodal point in the European exchange of both material goods and ideas, made it exceptionally susceptible to the spread of Reformation ideologies.[15]

These opposition movements reached revolutionary heights in the late 1560s, and by 1588 the Dutch Republic had been formed. Though the merchant and bourgeois elements were dominant in the cities before this, they had been subordinated to and constrained by local and foreign feudal ruling classes. After the revolution, the bourgeoisie *were* the ruling class.

England was an even clearer example. The cause of the Parliamentarians in the Civil War of the 1640s was tied up with the defence of Protestantism against a feared resurgence of Catholicism and feudal absolutism.[16] The execution of King Charles I and the subsequent establishment of the republican Commonwealth was perhaps the single most influential event of the modern era. The Enlightenment, the immediate forerunner of the liberal tradition, was more than anything else a project of interpreting the events of the English Revolution.

---

15. Brandon 2007, *"Popular Reformation"*.
16. Manning 1991, pp.72–101.

Compromise and tolerance

Oliver Cromwell, the leader of the English Parliamentarians and then Lord Protector of the Commonwealth, was not known as a tolerant man. In all ways representative of the vanguard of the proto-bourgeois "middling sort of men", Cromwell was personally and politically a zealous Puritan, and after the war he executed thousands of Irish in the name of ending "popery" (though, of course, there were other, more worldly, reasons for his regime to consolidate power over Ireland).

In the revolutionary period then, at least in England, the question of religious freedom or tolerance was not high on the agenda of the leading bourgeois forces. But for the Enlightenment tradition, and subsequently for liberalism, religious tolerance (and later, secularism) was of central importance.

There is certainly a basis for these ideas in the logic of abstract capital. The formal equality inherent in the commodity form suggests an indifference to faith, and the revolutionising of the means of production in general requires that, at a minimum, religious dogmas should not hinder the pursuit of rational material sciences.

But since religious freedom was not necessarily a part of the bourgeois revolutionary program in the early seventeenth century, it is worth trying to understand what historical processes led to its inclusion as part of the liberal tradition.

After Cromwell's death, the republican government floundered and was overthrown by Royalist forces. The monarchy that was "restored" was fundamentally different from that which had come before, as can be seen in King Charles II's *Declaration of Breda*, which concedes important powers to the parliament.[17] It was the 1688 "Glorious Revolution", though, that established the great compromise: the state would be wielded in the interests of the bourgeoisie, and the aristocracy could keep their property and political positions so long as they did not conspire to turn back the clock.

For the bourgeoisie, such a compromise was not counterposed to their victory. The main obstacle to the further development of capitalism, after all, had been the superstructural institutions of the

---

17. British House of Lords 1660, "*The King's Declaration*".

aristocracy – the feudal state. With that obstacle cleared out of the way, the bourgeoisie could make further inroads through economic means, safe in the knowledge that they would control the institutions of power in any future political conflicts.

There was another great pressure which pushed the bourgeoisie towards compromise – the lower elements of the popular classes. In the English Civil War there emerged political projects that went beyond the bounds of what the bourgeois forces were willing to countenance. The most famous were the programs of the Levellers, who campaigned for universal suffrage, and the more marginal Diggers, who called for the abolition of property altogether.

In light of this more fundamental threat, those forces of the bourgeoisie that had only reluctantly supported the revolution changed their strategy. As Albert Weisbord puts it:

> The progress of the Civil Wars had revealed what a small proportion of the population they actually constituted. They hastened, then, to make peace with all possible elements, whether royalist or democratic.[18]

This entailed religious tolerance of the different Protestant denominations that made up these various forces. A slightly more thorough religious tolerance (it included Jews to an extent, but still proscribed reactionary Catholics) was enacted in the Dutch Republic after the end of the political and religious conflicts of the Thirty Years War in 1648.

It was in this context, in 1689, that John Locke penned *A Letter Concerning Toleration*, in which he states:

> This narrowness of Spirit on all sides has undoubtedly been the principal Occasion of our Miseries and Confusions. But whatever have been the Occasion, it is now high time to seek for a thorow Cure... Since you are pleased to inquire what are my Thoughts about the mutual Toleration of Christians in their different Professions of Religion, I must needs answer you freely, That I

---

18.   Weisbord 1937, "*I. The English Civil Wars: 4*".

esteem that Toleration to be the chief Characteristical Mark of the True Church.[19]

Locke is a foundational thinker of the Enlightenment and, subsequently, the liberal tradition. That his desire for toleration comes from the experience of the English Civil Wars is explicitly laid out in the text. Thus, even the progenitors of liberalism understood that their philosophies were not plucked from the ether but were developed in specific social and historical contexts.

Religious tolerance – which, it must be said, remained highly restrictive for much of liberalism's history – was one such historical development.

Against conservatism and radicalism

History also forced liberalism to define itself against rival political tendencies. This did not happen overnight, but was a messy process of developments inside of and against the mainstream liberal tradition. Ultimately, the main political traditions that liberalism defined itself in opposition to were conservatism and radicalism.

It can be argued that modern conservatism is a fundamentally liberal ideology. No conservative (at least since the halfway point of the nineteenth century) seriously wants to destroy capitalism and revert to feudal politics and economics. Conservatives are also just as likely as liberals to invoke key thinkers of the Enlightenment and liberal traditions to support their arguments.

But there are dynamics which put conservatism at odds with liberalism proper. It is true that they are both capitalist frameworks. In some ways, conservatism is the more pragmatic framework of the bourgeoisie. If liberalism is the perspective of abstract capital, conservatism can perhaps be said to be the perspective of actually existing capital, concerned with the dirty business of ruling. Thus private property is sacrosanct for conservatives, but on freedom, rights, and formal equality the tradition is much more ambivalent. For a conservative, order is much more important than these airy ideals.

---

19.   Locke 1689, "*To the reader*".

At some point, then, the philosophies of the bourgeoisie developed in (at least) two different directions. The development of conservatism is easy enough to understand – once capitalism has conquered its feudal forerunners, the main purpose of politics is to justify that victory and defeat threats to that position. The two-sided nature of the bourgeois ideology in the revolutionary period gave way to a more one-sided approach as the threat of feudal counter-revolution receded.

But the developing split with liberalism was not made explicit until social processes forced them into view. Most central was the revolutionary process of the late eighteenth century – the American Revolution, and particularly the French Revolution. Both revolutions were fought under the banner of identifiably liberal ideas, and although the French Revolution wavered first left and then right, the ultimate settlement of both revolutions produced fundamentally liberal regimes.

The American and French Revolutions, coming later in the bourgeois revolutionary period, had the benefit of learning from the previous examples. In both cases, the transmission belt of ideas is quite clear. Enlightenment thought, informed by the Dutch Revolt and English Civil War, was widely discussed in the salons of France, and by the drafters of the American Declaration of Independence.

There are plenty of texts which have accurately demonstrated the hypocrisies of the liberalism of the American revolutionaries. The first section of Domenico Losurdo's book *Liberalism: A Counter-History* is a compendium of evidence that early American liberals never took the question of slavery seriously. Losurdo says this is because "'class interests' – principally of those who owned large plantations and a considerable number of slaves – played an important role".[20] This is true enough, but requires some additional explanation.

Conservatism implicitly existed at this time. In fact, Edmund Burke, who is rightly considered the father of conservatism, professed sympathy with the aims of the Americans (though never with their actual struggle).[21] The American bourgeoisie, though, did not take up a conservative framework in its struggle against British rule. Their project was distinctly *liberal*, not just capitalist.

---

20.   Losurdo 2011, p.30.
21.   Burke 1775, "*Speech On Moving His Resolutions For Conciliation With The Colonies*".

Liberalism was the framework of the American revolutionaries because it provided something for their social project. It was a political philosophy that fitted capitalist existence, yes, but one that particularly fitted *their* capitalist existence. The American bourgeoisie, unlike the English, needed to throw off the restrictions of their colonial overlord in order to fully realise their own capitalist development. The ideas of liberalism were useful tools for this project, as they have been for many similar projects since. Additionally, liberal ideas could motivate other class forces dissatisfied with British rule to fight alongside the more outright bourgeois ones.

Simultaneously, the central freedom that the Americans fought for was obviously the freedom of property owners. This is the real crux of the matter with slavery, as Losurdo correctly points out. It is worth considering, though, the positive side of the American Revolution, and particularly how it contributed to the formulation of modern liberalism.

The American Revolution was not one of the bourgeoisie overthrowing feudalism, but a budding national bourgeoisie overthrowing a restrictive capitalist overlord: a bourgeois revolution against another section of the bourgeoisie. This dynamic meant the thinkers had to define themselves against a rival capitalist philosophy. Although there was a previous ideological struggle inside the Enlightenment tradition between more liberal and more conservative thinkers, the revolutionary process in America started to solidify a tradition that was distinct from the dominant politics in England.

The distinction between liberalism and conservatism, though, is made clear in response to the much deeper revolutionary process that shook France, starting in 1789. Unlike the American Revolution, in which the masses never played more than an auxiliary role, in France the Parisian artisans and proto-working class asserted themselves from the beginning of the revolution.

At first, the liberal wing of the revolution was not primarily hostile to these layers. A kind of uneasy alliance existed between the bourgeois revolutionaries and the popular masses who were mobilised against the old regime. It is hard to imagine how the liberal forces could have come to power without the storming of the Bastille, or the women's march on Versailles.

Nonetheless, the liberal leadership of the revolution was not oblivious to the threat that the masses could get beyond their control. Less than a fortnight after the women's march, they instituted martial law to prevent future mobilisations.

On the other side, the liberal forces were up against the reactionaries. The king and his family attempted to flee the country many times, and rumours of aristocratic conspiracies against the new government circulated widely. It was primarily this that forced the liberals into more decisive action against the old order.

When the aristocratic ruling classes of the rest of Europe intervened militarily into France to aid the counter-revolution, the dynamics of the ensuing war pushed the liberals out of power. Their commitment to compromise and tolerance had run up against the realities of an obstinate aristocracy on one side and the adamant popular masses on the other. Paris would eventually fall under the political leadership of Maximilien Robespierre and the Jacobins.

Much could be said about the political project of the Jacobins. It will suffice for our purposes to recognise that there were differences within this political current (and Robespierre's politics themselves were not static), but Jacobinism can broadly be understood as the hard left of the bourgeois revolutionary tradition – a kind of bourgeois radicalism.

The Jacobins oversaw the period of the Terror, which still today remains the bogeyman of both conservatives and liberals. The Terror was a campaign of arrests and execution of those who were considered traitors or threats to the revolution. While later, when the bourgeois radicalism of Robespierre had also run up against its limits, it was turned against the left, the primary motivation for the Terror was to end the counter-revolution of the aristocracy, the Church and agents for foreign powers. It was also in this period that the masses forced the government to institute price controls for basic goods such as bread, thus impinging upon the rights of the free market.

Though it was written in 1790, before the Terror solidified conservative opinion against the revolution, Edmund Burke's *Reflections on the Revolution in France* was a clear-sighted conservative argument for a hostility to the French Revolution, to revolutions in general, and to liberalism's part in such processes. In this text, Burke rewrites the history of the English Revolution by asserting that the English constitution of 1688 was "in its fundamental principles for ever settled" (as if a revolution had not settled it), and declaring that the rights of the "subject" cannot exist without the monarchy, as they are "bound indissolubly together".[22] This allows him to go on to attack the French Revolution as completely unlike that of his own country.

Burke's political attacks on the women's march on Versailles are obviously consistent with the philosophy laid out in *Reflections*, as is his open support of the monarchy and the reactionary Catholic Church. Burke developed conservatism, then, specifically with the formulation that liberals undermine their own political project; that by questioning *any* social order they undermine social order in general.

So, Burke was explicit that despite some propertied classes supporting the revolution, the dynamic would threaten the right of property in general. As Neil Davidson puts it, "Burke understood, from very early in the process, the logic of escalation that would come to dominate the revolution and drive it further than the bourgeoisie intended".[23]

In later years, liberalism would denounce the "excesses" of the French Revolution. Conservatism, following Burke's lead, denounced the entire process, including the role played by the liberals.

Eventually, the most radical phase of the French Revolution was restrained by more moderate bourgeois forces, who in turn handed the reins over to Napoleon. The Napoleonic era, and the short restoration of the Bourbon royal family afterwards, was one of internal counter-revolution. But it should not be understood that this counter-revolution overturned the newly forged capitalist state, let alone capitalist relations in France. It was a period of reactionary conservatism, but on a bourgeois basis, not a feudal one.

So, by 1830, when another revolution overthrew the restored Bourbons, the liberals found themselves wedged between two political projects they detested. On the right, the threat of capitalist but reactionary politics that ran counter to the fundamentals of freedom, rights and equality. On the left, the radicals (some of whom would soon describe themselves as "socialist") threatened to undermine the very

---

22. Burke 1790, p.8.
23. Davidson 2012, p.78.

basis of the new order – private property. Of these, it was clear which the liberals feared more.

Thus the arch-liberal Lafayette, who had been a general in George Washington's army and then drafted the *Declaration of the Rights of Man and of the Citizen* during the French Revolution, decided to pledge his loyalty to a Bourbon cousin, so that the monarchy could protect liberty against the threat of social disorder:

> Monsieur de Lafayette, realising the assembly's growing indecision, suddenly charged himself with renouncing the Presidency: he handed the Duc d'Orléans a tricolour flag, advanced onto the balcony of the Hôtel de Ville, and embraced the Prince in full view of the astonished crowd, while the latter waved the national flag. Lafayette's republican kiss made a king. A strange ending to the life of the hero of Two Worlds![24]

Liberalism had spawned both conservatism and radicalism. Conservatives, though, at least after capitalism had thoroughly conquered state power, were not a fundamental threat to the capitalist class basis of liberalism. Individuals within the radical tradition, on the other hand, took the abstract principles of liberalism so seriously that they came to the (correct) conclusion that private property was a barrier to their realisation.

Gracchus Babeuf, who was executed in 1797 by the counter-revolutionary regime in France, took these politics the farthest: "Babeuf usually described his position as the advocacy of 'true equality' or 'common happiness'. But his aim of a society based on economic equality and common ownership of property is clearly recognisable as what later became known as socialism".[25]

Insofar as radicalism did question private property, it marked a break with the liberal tradition. This break was necessarily limited, though, before a different class could be found on which radical politics could base itself.

---

24. de Chateaubriand, *BkXXXII:Chap15:Sec1*.
25. Birchall 1996.

Democracy and social liberalism

In the nineteenth century, the working class emerged as a political force. It was, as Marx put it, a "class with radical chains".[26] The perspective of the working class allowed for a totally different kind of politics from liberalism. The social position of this class, as a propertyless and collective class, laid the basis for a radical politics that could overcome the paradoxes that liberal radicalism remained mired in.

Ever since the working class was first constituted as a social layer, their struggles had impacted liberalism. We have seen how the earliest proto-working class movements were important in pushing radicalism to its limits in France. But with the consolidation of capitalism, the working class grew in numbers and political importance. Historically, it was the struggles of the working class that forced liberalism to formulate its positions on two important themes: democracy and the "social question" (inequality and exploitation; basically, class).

There had always been a strand in liberalism that supported democracy and the "general good" of humanity. The Levellers in the English Civil War, for instance, campaigned for universal suffrage, without opposing property rights. The democratic forces, though, were a smaller opposition to Cromwell's more mainstream bourgeois politics of limiting the vote to property holders. In the French Revolution, the liberal phase from 1789–91 gave the vote only to "active citizens" of property, and it was only under the more radical National Convention of 1792 that universal male suffrage was introduced.

The democratic tradition of these forces, despite being opposed to the mainstream, did not break fundamentally with liberalism. Theirs was a framework which supported universal male suffrage and a redistribution of wealth to the poor, but within the logic of liberal philosophy. Thomas Paine is a fitting example, particularly in his most radical work, *Rights of Man – Part Second, Combining Principle and Practice.*

Paine in this text denounces all hereditary offices, supports universal suffrage, and even goes so far as to suggest that: "When, in countries that are called civilised, we see age going to the workhouse and youth to the gallows, something must be wrong in the system of

---

26.   Marx 1843, *"Introduction"*.

government".[27] His conclusion is to distribute wealth to the poor, and he spends pages detailing how this could be done (reducing military spending, rationalising government offices, clearing out corruption).

All this was a challenge to the mainstream of liberalism at the time, certainly, but Paine's reasons for supporting both democracy and social welfare were liberal ones. Individualism, rights, and formal equality were the starting point. Indeed, Paine was quite explicit in *Rights of Man* that these values came from the commodity form itself:

> The invention of commerce...is the greatest approach towards universal civilisation that has yet been made... Commerce is no other than the traffic of two individuals, multiplied on a scale of numbers; and by the same rule that nature intended for the intercourse of two, she intended that of all.[28]

Ultimately, it was that great historical test, the Reign of Terror, which proved that Paine was incapable of breaking with liberalism. He disavowed the radicals' execution of the royal family, denounced the influence that "Paris" (read: the radical *sans-culottes*) had on the government, and opposed price controls.[29] That is to say, despite being abstractly for democracy and social equality, he opposed the concrete measures that went the furthest in this direction in Paris.

Despite this opposition to Jacobin radicalism, Paine's ideas were still seen as too radical by many liberals. His democratic and social ideals remained outside the mainstream of liberalism until the working class threatened to find their own path to democracy and equality.

The practice of liberalism in the nineteenth century was a backward step from the heights of Paine. The 1848 revolution in France, and then the period of radical reconstruction after the Civil War in America, saw liberal forces at first fight for democracy and social justice, only to later compromise with conservatives against threats to private property, the nation or social order. So in France, the liberals crushed

---

27. Paine 1779–92, *Chapter V, "Ways and means of improving the condition of Europe interspersed with miscellaneous observations"*.
28. Paine 1793.
29. Paine 1793.

the workers' uprising in June and then accommodated themselves to Louis Napoleon's dictatorship. In America, those liberals who had been against slavery (many liberals had actually defended the South's right to "liberty") allowed the rise of the Ku Klux Klan and Jim Crow segregation in the South.

By the turn of the twentieth century, though, a new current had emerged. In Britain, the "social liberal" philosophy of John Stuart Mill was beginning to gather a following. A similar project would later become mainstream to American liberalism. Both had similarities to Paine, but were much more informed by working-class politics.

Matt McManus has claimed that Mill can be understood as a social-ist, partly because of his self-identification as such.[30] The politics that he articulates, though, fail to go beyond liberalism and thus fail to challenge capitalism.

Firstly, it is important to state that insofar as democratic and/or social liberalism were ever taken up by sections of the ruling class, it was for two reasons: fear of the class struggle, and to justify specific economic changes that were beneficial to capitalism.

In Britain, the history of the early nineteenth century was one of thunderous working-class revolts for the vote, reaching its height with the Chartist rebellion in 1839. The revolt was so serious that one British general feared an insurrection, and was not confident in his ability to put it down if it eventuated.[31] These struggles caused some sections of liberal politics to consider introducing universal suffrage so as to prevent social revolution. This project was implemented piece-meal over the next half-century, by liberals who won the support of a defeated and more politically moderate working class.

British capitalism had also developed by the twentieth century to the point where it was beneficial for capitalism to have an educated workforce. For the purposes of social discipline and technical instruc-tion, schooling was expanded. The state, having invested resources into educating workers, was also compelled to keep them alive and able to work for as long as possible, and thus health care and welfare accorded also with this period.

---

30. McManus 2021.
31. Foot 2006, p.100.

The ruling class more broadly, then, was open to the ideological arguments that the social liberals were making. This was never uncontested, though, and part of the eventual acceptance of social liberalism into the liberal mainstream in the twentieth century was the process of political demarcation against its insistent conservative rival.

It is useful to return to Mill briefly, as an example of the limits of a politics that fails to break with liberalism. Mill's politics are in some ways more radical than Thomas Paine's (though not really in his practice – Mill was a true believer in reforms rather than radical struggle). He was an early proponent of women's suffrage, denounced the power of the capitalist class over politics, and articulated support for workers' control of their workplaces. Nevertheless, his program is utopian, while simultaneously failing to go beyond the bounds of capitalism.

The core of the problem is that Mill accepts private property, and merely seeks to make workers the collective owners of that private property via a system of worker cooperatives.[32] Thus, in Mill's formulations, competition and private property remain.[33] This means that Mill's framework cannot deal with the problems of the anarchy of capitalist competition, or the subsequent economic crises.

Mill is also fundamentally elitist, which leads him to an anti-working class prejudice against democracy and racist support for colonialism. This elitism also informs an attitude that the current form of the state could be a positive good, if only the corrupting influence of individual capitalists could be purged from it. For Mill, the state must educate the workers, to make them morally virtuous enough to accept socialism, while administering their health care and welfare from on high.

All this is consistent with liberalism as the perspective of abstract capital. Like Paine, Mill is able to articulate support for democratic rights and social justice using liberal values. But his framework accepts the commodity form at a fundamental level, and also maintains the need for a minority state that maintains the monopoly of violence over

---

32.   Mill 1870, *Chapter VII: "On the probable futurity of the labouring classes"*, §6.
33.   Mill 1879, *"The Socialist Objections to the Present Order of Society Examined"*.

both individuals and the masses (such force, remember, is required for generalised commodity production).

In short, the social liberalism of Mill does not reject the perspective of abstract capital for the perspective of the working class, but instead seeks to put workers in the position of abstract capital. This is an impossibility in the real world, and so the grand, lofty ideas of Mill are instead used to justify the pittances of liberal welfare state politics.

Both Paine, who takes the abstract values of liberalism to their most radical conclusion, and Mill, who is strongly influenced by working-class politics, fail to break with the fundamentals of the liberal framework. Failing to reject the perspective of abstract capital, and accepting as natural the commodity form, means their politics are incapable of challenging the fundamentals of capitalism.

Conclusion

For the purposes of this article, I have attempted to focus on the foundational properties of liberalism. This has meant leaving aside much that is worthy of discussion – most glaringly the development of liberalism in the twentieth century, and the emergence of particular bourgeois political traditions, such as reactionary nationalism and fascism. Nonetheless, I believe that the framework provided here can help to illuminate liberalism's relationship to these developments.

An understanding of liberalism is necessary for Marxists, mostly in order to politically combat it. Despite the many twists and turns of the liberal tradition, it has not escaped its fundamental basis in abstract capital. Because of this, any innovation in liberalism is trapped within the capitalist framework, regardless of what the theorists who come up with those innovations might think.

Liberalism, as the perspective of abstract capital, inherits the contradictions of the commodity form. Freedom, enforced by authority; rights, for property and its owners; and formal equality, which must by definition ignore the reality of material inequality.

The framework of liberalism was not handed down from God. Nor was it, as liberals are more likely to suggest, some pre-existing supra-historical truth that was "discovered". Liberalism was developed by human beings in specific social contexts. That is to say, liberalism is developed and utilised by specific (bourgeois) class forces.

Early bourgeois thought developed inside feudalism, and was articulated by the social forces involved using the existing frameworks. The Renaissance dressed itself in a Roman toga, and the Protestant Reformation claimed its authority from the Bible. Nonetheless, these relatively half-formed ideas proved capable of politically arming revolutions such as the Dutch Revolt and the English Civil War.

These early revolutions revealed the Janus-faced nature of the rising bourgeoisie: restricted by the old feudal order on one side and threatened by the popular masses on the other. Once in power, the bourgeoisie compromised with the defeated aristocracy and eventually liberalism produced its sibling, bourgeois conservatism, in order to maintain social order.

The high revolutionary period of the late eighteenth century forced liberalism to identify itself against this conservatism, and then against the more dire threat of bourgeois radicalism. Opposition to the politics of both reactionaries and radicals became definitional to the liberal tradition.

By the mid-nineteenth century, liberalism was more or less codified. Chartism and the 1848 revolutions would turn liberalism thoroughly against revolutionary means, and the later acceptance of democratic rights was in pursuit of this anti-revolutionary goal. Social liberalism was similarly informed by working-class politics, and even then was only taken up by mainstream liberalism when its most tame policies became beneficial for capital accumulation.

The social basis and the history of liberalism makes it clear that there is nothing to be redeemed in these politics. Liberals might honestly support freedom and equality, but these ideals cannot be achieved while capitalism reigns. Marxism, on the other hand, can explain why liberalism is incapable of fulfilling its own aims. Ultimately, only a Marxist framework is capable of politically arming the struggle against the quandaries of bourgeois philosophy and politics, against the reality of world capitalism, and for the liberation of humanity.

References

Barker, Colin 2019, "Revolutionary reflections | Value, force, many states and other problems: part 2", *Revolutionary Socialism in the 21st Century* (rs21). https://revsoc21.uk/2019/05/24/revolutionary-reflections-value-force-many-states-and-other-problems-part-2/

Birchall, Ian 1996, "The Babeuf Bicentenary: Conspiracy or Revolutionary Party?", *International Socialism*, 2:72, September. https://www.marxists.org/history/etol/writers/birchall/1996/xx/babeuf.htm

Brandon, Pepijn 2007, "The Dutch Revolt: a social analysis" *International Socialism, 116, Autumn*. https://isj.org.uk/the-dutch-revolt-a-social-analysis/

British House of Lords 1660, "House of Lords Journal", Vol. 11, *British History Online*. https://www.british-history.ac.uk/lords-jrnl/vol11/pp6-9#h3-0009

Burke, Edmund 1775, "The Works of the Right Honourable Edmund Burke", *Project Gutenberg*. https://www.gutenberg.org/files/15198/15198-h/15198-h.htm

Burke, Edmund 1790, "Reflections on the Revolution in France", *Early Modern Texts*. https://www.earlymoderntexts.com/assets/pdfs/burke1790part1.pdf

de Chateaubriand, François 1849 [trans. AS Kline 2005], *Poetry in Translation*. https://www.poetryintranslation.com/PITBR/Chateaubriand/ChateaubriandMemoirsBookXXXII.php

Davidson, Neil 2012, *How Revolutionary Were the Bourgeois Revolutions?*, *Haymarket Books*.

Foot, Paul 2006, *The Vote: How it Was Won and How it Was Undermined*, Penguin.

Harman, Chris 1989, "From feudalism to capitalism", *International Socialism*, 2:45, Winter, pp.35–87. https://www.marxists.org/archive/harman/1989/xx/transition.html

Hobbes, Thomas 1651, *Leviathan, Project Gutenberg*. https://www.gutenberg.org/files/3207/3207-h/3207-h.htm

Locke, John 1689, "A Letter Concerning Toleration", *Online Library of Liberty*. *https://oll.libertyfund.org/titles/goldie-a-letter-concerning-toleration-and-other-writings*

Locke, John 1690, *Second Treatise of Government, Project Gutenberg*. *https://www.gutenberg.org/files/7370/7370-h/7370-h.htm*

Losurdo, Domenic 2011, *Liberalism: A Counter-History*, Verso.

Machiavelli, Niccolo 1513, *Discourses on the First Ten Books of Titus Livius*, *Marxists Internet Archive*. https://www.marxists.org/reference/archive/machiavelli/works/discourses/index.htm

Manning, Brian 1991 [1976], *The English People and the English Revolution*, Bookmarks.

Marx, Karl 1843, *Critique of Hegel's Philosophy of Right*, *Marxists Internet Archive*. https://www.marxists.org/archive/marx/works/1843/critique-hpr/index.htm

Marx, Karl 1847, *Manifesto of the Communist Party*, *Marxists Internet Archive*. https://www.marxists.org/archive/marx/works/1848/communist-manifesto/

Marx, Karl 1867, *Capital*, Vol. I, *Marxists Internet Archive*. https://www.marxists.org/archive/marx/works/1867-c1/

McManus, Matt 2021, "Was John Stuart Mill a Socialist?", *Jacobin, May 30*. https://jacobin.com/2021/05/john-stewart-js-mill-liberal-socialism-locke-madison

Mill, John Stuart 1870, "Principles of Political Economy", *Online Library of Liberty*. https://oll.libertyfund.org/titles/mill-principles-of-political-economy-ashley-ed

Mill, John Stuart 1879, "Socialism", *Project Gutenberg*. https://www.gutenberg.org/files/38138/38138-h/38138-h.htm

Paine, Thomas 1779–92, *The Writings of Thomas Paine*, Vol. II, *Project Gutenberg*. https://www.gutenberg.org/cache/epub/3742/pg3742-images.html

Paine, Thomas 1793, "Letter to Jacques Danton", *The Thomas Paine National Historical Association*. https://thomaspaine.org/works/letters/other/to-george-jacques-danton-may-6-1793.html

Pashukanis, Evgeny 1924, "The General Theory of Law and Marxism", *Marxists Internet Archive*. https://www.marxists.org/archive/pashukanis/1924/law/

Weber, Max 1905, "The Protestant Ethic and the Spirit of Capitalism", *Marxists Internet Archive*. https://www.marxists.org/reference/archive/weber/protestant-ethic/index.htm

Weisbord, Albert 1937, *Conquest of Power. Book 1: Liberalism*, The Albert & Vera Weisbord Archives, *Marxists Internet Archive*. https://www.marxists.org/archive/weisbord/conquest1.htm

LIZ ROSS

Review: The rise and fall of union power in the Pilbara

Liz Ross is the author of *Dare to Struggle, Dare to Win, Builders Labourers fight deregistration, 1981–94* and *Stuff the Accord! Pay Up! Workers' resistance to the ALP-ACTU Accord.*

Striking Ore. The rise and fall of union power in the Pilbara, Alexis Vassiley, Monash University Press 2025

I F WE ARE to rebuild a fighting working class capable of winning a society run in the interests of the many and not the few, then it's essential to know and understand the history of class struggle, both the victories and defeats.

Striking Ore is an impressive contribution to such an endeavour. Focused on a key industry in the Australian economy, iron ore mining, it traces how rank-and-file militancy built nearly 100 percent unionisation in the harsh mining region of the Pilbara in northern Western Australia in the 1960s and 1970s. Through first-hand accounts of the unionists and extensive research, the book traces how the whole region was transformed for both the workers and their families. Then, it details the devastating impact of the class-collaborationist ACTU-ALP Accord (1983–96) which largely de-unionised the Pilbara and handed workplace power to the employers, as reliance on the courts and legality stripped workers of their power on the job. Finally, the book takes us to the results today, where a Fly-In-Fly-Out (FIFO) workforce, with only 5 percent unionisation (national rate is 12.5 percent), works punishing hours in poor conditions, while industry profits have boomed. Seeing the highest of the highs and lowest of the lows, Pilbara unionism mirrors Australia's recent union history in an "exaggerated and time-compressed form".[1]

In concluding, Vassiley argues that strategies based on "both strengths and weaknesses...from the heyday of union power in the Pilbara mines...offer a way forward". He discusses rank-and-file unionism, the role of the trade union bureaucracy, various union strategies such as the "Organising Model", through to the need for a clear class politics to prepare us for the task facing us today. That is, to rebuild a layer of union activists committed to fighting for a militant class-struggle strategy within our unions.

Iron ore mining came late to the Pilbara. It wasn't until the 1930s that large-scale mining and export were attempted, only to be halted over the potential war with Japan and predicted ore shortages.[2] By 1960, when the scope of the deposits in WA's Kimberley region was realised and Cold War pressures eased, the ban was lifted and the first shipment left the Pilbara in 1966.

At this stage, most of the power lay with management. Unlike the long history of union organisation in the rest of Australia, effectively unions had to start from scratch in the Pilbara. And they did.

The unions began by sending in organisers for weeks at a time, signing up members and establishing a branch to elect their own shop stewards. Where a job site was covered by a number of unions, combined union shop committees were also formed – a key development in building the solidarity necessary to tackle the employers. After this boost from Perth-based officials, it was then up to the local organisation to build the union. In the late 1960s, after Australian Workers Union (AWU) organiser Gil Barr "fronted the company" to get three workers reinstated, Mount Newman's 400-strong workforce began to

---

1.   All quotes from *Striking Ore*.
2.   At the time it was estimated that Australia had only 264 million tonnes of iron ore reserves, likely to run out within 25 years. Today the Pilbara is one of the biggest iron ore deposits in the world, with the 2025 discovery of a single record-breaking 55 billion metric tonne deposit worth $6 trillion.

join the union. "From then on", he says "we started to get membership as the guys could see the benefit of it".

As well, the political and industrial situation was changing, both internationally and in Australia. Nationwide, by the late 1960s industrial action was ramping up, coming to a spectacular peak when there was a partial general strike over the jailing of tramways union leader Clarrie O'Shea for refusing to pay a fine for striking. Western Australian unions, including those from three Pilbara mines, struck, pulling out up to 100,000 workers across almost all sectors. During 1969 disputes over sackings, working conditions and site allowances spread across Pilbara's mines and ports, with industrial action largely run by the shop stewards and rank-and-file members. Strikes, lasting between one day and four months, delivered significant gains.

It was an ongoing battle though, with gains won in one mine having to be fought for in the next, but with each win setting a benchmark. To achieve that outcome, as Randall Grant, AWU shop steward at Hamersley Iron's Dampier port, pointed out, "We had industrial muscle and we used it". Their workplace meetings were more often about going on strike than discussing general union affairs. The result was that by the early 1970s these workers had curbed the worst excesses of management and through militant action won improved wages and conditions.

Workers and their shop steward and combined union structures had succeeded in shifting the always present workplace "frontier of control" between the bosses and workers, in the unions' favour. Workers themselves decided recruitment, discipline and staffing matters, as well as enforcing safety standards, usually seen as management's fiefdom. Union influence also spread to workers' lives at home, turning company towns into union towns where housing, sporting facilities, food, health care and many other aspects of life thrived. AWU shop steward Harry Hoskin recalls: "The union was a big part of my life...some of the best years... The work...was just you turn up and crush rocks", but the sports and other improvements in the townships "really made it for me".

This grassroots union power, however, was a thorn in the companies' sides and was a growing concern for the union bureaucracy as it sought a more rules-based, legalistic resolution of industrial relations.[3] A major 10-week dispute in 1979 at Hamersly Iron saw clashes not just between the company and workers, but also between the Perth-based union officials and the ACTU and the grassroots committees which were running the dispute.

The dispute turned national after the state Liberal government, backed by its counterpart in Canberra, used anti-union laws to arrest workers and top union officials. Two million workers around the country held a 24-hour strike, which while it expanded support for the Hamersley Iron workers, shifted control of the dispute towards the union officials and the courts. The bureaucracy's entry, as Vassiley notes, foreshadowed its increasing involvement in the region through-out the 1980s, magnified from 1983 when the class-collaborationist politics of the ALP-ACTU Accord led to the destruction of rank-and-file organising.

Nonetheless, boom times in 1980–81 seemed to counter that trend as workers smashed through wages and conditions barriers. But 1982 saw one of the sharpest worldwide economic downturns, followed by a stampede of restraint by reformist forces to save capitalism from itself. The Accord promised wage moderation and social safety nets for workers while ensuring company profits would rise.

The shock of the downturn, the sudden defeats and the loss of working-class confidence, allowed the union bureaucracy to expand its influence on the job through such structures as industry plans managed by tripartite consultative bodies which undercut rank-and-file agency. The Pilbara Iron Ore Industry Consultative Council's brief was to study international iron ore trade and Australia's role. By exaggerating the economic challenges from countries such as Brazil, the IOICC corralled unions into endless meetings, overseas conferences and "fact-finding" missions, all emphasising the needs of profit, while constantly calling for workers' industrial restraint to meet these challenges. Management's "poisoned handshake" approach

---

3.   At the height of rank-and-file control in the Pilbara, an organiser had flown in, talked to management and only called a members' meeting the next day. In the pub afterwards one of the workers slapped down the price of a beer on the counter, telling the organiser: "That's your fucking redundancy money, grab it and fuck off".

aimed to improve productivity and efficiency, was how one participant explained it. Amalgamated Metal Workers Union (AMWU) Convener Garry Kruger saw it as "a pile of shit... I think it was an appeasement by the companies... It was more of a talk shop, always reminded me of *The Life of Brian*".

As the Accord policies were implemented, unions around the country were under attack from Labor and the top union layers. Small unions like the Food Preservers Union, glass workers and isolated abattoirs covered by the meatworkers' union came under enormous pressure to toe the line on wages and conditions and giving up the right to strike. While unions were often threatened with deregistration, massive fines and the like, the government took the extreme step of mobilising the airforce to destroy the pilots' union. Another of the damaging onslaughts was the deregistration of the Builders Labourers Federation (BLF) in 1986.[4] With the backing of most of the union movement, the BLF was denied coverage – and its members' jobs – because their flouting of the Accord's restraint threatened Labor's restructuring and revival of capitalism.

That same year, the Pilbara's most militant workforce at Robe River was under siege. Between June 1986 and January 1987 says Vassiley, "union power was destroyed, hundreds of unionists had left, there were no full-time convenors and shop stewards were no longer recognised. Work practices built up over decades – ensuring safety, reducing work intensity and preserving jobs and good working conditions – were taken away".

Even at the time, everyone knew that knocking off Robe River would mean unions were finished in the Pilbara. AWU Convenor Peter Hollow put it bluntly: "If they can knock off the Pilbara they'll knock off everywhere else. And they did".

New management by Peko-Wallsend, under the leadership of "New Right" ideologue Charles Copeman, confronted the unions head on. Conducting a four-stage operation, the company started with a major work restructure and a one-third cut in jobs, and all union agreements, formal and informal, were abolished. Wilfully ignoring

---

4.   See Ross 2004.

Industrial Commission orders and agreements, Copeman then cut a swathe through the workforce, enforced redundancies, jumbled up work rosters and job descriptions, then sacked those who refused to do work they had no experience or qualifications for. Strikes at Robe River were only held in the very last period – and only then sparked off by a Federated Engine Drivers and Firemen's Union (FEDFU) wildcat strike – when the ACTU promptly moved in to override the workers and sign off a "peace package" with Copeman. Striking was deemed to be playing into management's hands, and solidarity action from others in the Pilbara and around Australia was rejected on the grounds of vulnerability to crippling fines. Instead of a retaliatory full-scale fightback by the unions, their leadership led workers down the path of management and court-brokered resolutions, public relations campaigns and lobbying governments. And defeat.

It could have been very different. Cape Lambert Electrical Trades Union (ETU) chair Graeme Haynes outlines the union's strengths which could have beaten back Copeman:

> [T]he real strength of the union movement is the rank-and-file membership, and it was never stronger at the time. We had close to 100 per cent membership, an excellent Combined Union Council, healthy strike funds, a long history of industrial action dating back to our first industrial agreement registered in 1972 – an agreement which became a Pilbara benchmark for other sites to progressively build on – a long history of industrial and financial support of fellow Pilbara unionists and their campaigns, and we had corresponding commitments from the other Pilbara Combined Union Councils at the commencement of the New Right attack on us.

Robe River was the beginning of the end, though not the final chapter. When Mount Newman management attempted a similar strategy two years later, using the very tactics rejected at Robe River, workers struck and defeated the anti-union drive. De-unionisation at Newman wasn't achieved until 1999, though other mines fell earlier. And on it went through the 1980s and 1990s till the region became a bastion of individually contracted, non-union FIFO employees, a hell for workers again and a bonanza of profits for the companies.

The long history of the Accord years, with defeat following defeat and a downward trajectory of union membership, strikes, wages and conditions, may seem puzzlingly the opposite of the promises. After all, it was meant to strengthen workers and their unions, provide an economy that could reward and protect workers from the vicissitudes of capital's boom and bust. And yet the rewards went to the ruling class while the workers found themselves de-unionised and experiencing real falls in wages and conditions, living a more precarious life.[5]

So why did it end up this way? And how can we turn things around? *Striking Ore*, with its detailed examination of the Pilbara region, is a crucial contribution to this discussion.

Throughout the Accord years, those who argued for militancy and solidarity were, like Graeme Haynes, called saboteurs, stooges of the New Right, risking the union's finances, or worse, members' jobs, even houses. These weren't just abusive name-calling, they were part of a political battle to shut down and discredit the militants and entrench the power of the bureaucracy. As FEDFU official Dick Keegan argued, the rank and file "were of little use" in what was the rightful realm of the bureaucracy, who "are changed under the Industrial Relations Act with the responsibility of administering the award and all industrial activities on site".

Members were told that the traditional ways were no longer suited to the economic policies of the day. Instead, as the Communist Party and Left Labor proponents argued, unions would be involved in the running of the economy through tripartite industry committees and the like. AMWU official Max Ogden claimed: "What we are witnessing is the development of the Australian union movement as a major political weapon...".

In fact, the AMWU had spent some years beforehand systematically educating their shop stewards in the politics of Accord-like class collaboration through regular forums and a widely-distributed set of booklets. What was needed was political arguments and organisation

---

5.   See Bramble 2008, Humphrys 2018 and Ross 2020 for further analysis of the Accord.

against the Accord and here workers were ill-prepared. Where there was opposition, it was mostly limited to ad hoc, albeit militant, resistance and not through an organised political alternative to the Accord. Attempts to build an organised opposition were valiant, but came after the Accord was implemented and faced the combined weight of the union movement and a Labor government prepared to go to any length to enforce it.

Since the Accord years Australian unions have tried various – mostly top-down – models to rebuild. Some, such as the Organising Model, did recruit new members, but then didn't develop those gains into more effective unions. Others, like the nurses, have held their numbers and a degree of militancy, while others fluctuate, gaining numbers when industrial action is taken, only to fall off as weak agreements are forced through. However despite being at record low levels, unionism is not dead in the Pilbara either, and the book rightly points to some of the rebuilding in the region. An inspiring success story is the Mining and Energy Union's campaign winning over 93 percent coverage among the train drivers and sealing a deal in 2024 that locks in major improvements in wages and conditions. In the mines themselves a combined Construction, Mining and Energy Union-AWU partnership, the Western Mine Workers' Alliance has not been as successful.

It means the last chapters in *Striking Ore* make for grim reading about working in the mines, with poor safety, wages and conditions, FIFO predominant and some shocking sexual harassment cases, all of which continue to today.

As detailed by Vassiley, the history of the Pilbara provides irrefutable proof of the success of rank-and-file organisation, where workers can shift the frontier of control in the workplace from the employer to greater worker control on the job. It shows how the interests of the union bureaucracy can move from backing and even leading workers in their struggles with the employers, to hog-tying the workers to legalities and the courts, stripping them of their industrial power. And why it is the officials' fundamental loyalty as reformists to protecting the interests of capitalism, developing class collaborationist policies such as the Accord and supporting draconian anti-union legislation, which "cannibalises" their own organisations.[6]

Fundamentally *Striking Ore* is an argument about the working-class politics necessary to rebuilding class-struggle unionism and ultimately a revolutionary change to society. It joins a small cohort of Marxist analyses that are essential in arming us with the political arguments we need.

References

Bramble, Tom 2008, *Trade unionism in Australia. A history from flood to ebb tide*, Cambridge University Press.

Humphrys, Elizabeth 2018, *How Labour built neoliberalism. Australia's Accord, the labour movement and the neoliberal project*, Haymarket Books.

Ross, Liz 2004, *Dare to Struggle, Dare to Win. Builders Labourers fight deregistration, 1981–94*, The Vulgar Press.

Ross, Liz 2020, , Interventions.

Vassiley, Alexis 2024, "Once more on the rank-and-file – union bureaucracy interplay: Mining unions", *Capital & Class*, Sage Journals. https://journals.sagepub.com/doi/10.1177/03098168241240462

---

6.   Vassiley develops this argument in Vassiley 2024.

JASMINE DUFF

Review: The origins of the modern police force and the socialist case for their overthrow

Jasmine Duff is an organiser for the Campaign Against Racism and Fascism. She has also been involved in campaigning for Palestine, climate justice, and organising Black Lives Matter rallies.

brian bean, *Their End is Our Beginning. Cops, Capitalism, and Abolition,* Haymarket Books, 2025.

TWO DAYS AFTER the fifth anniversary of the murder of George Floyd, 24-year-old Warlpiri man Kumanjayi White was killed by police in a Coles supermarket in Alice Springs. Weeks before, one of the same officers who killed White was photographed with his knee on the neck of an Aboriginal woman. The same police force that killed White was also responsible for the shooting of Kumanjayi Walker in 2019, and the coronial inquest into Walker's death found that Zachary Rolfe, the officer who murdered him, was "the beneficiary of an organisation with hallmarks of institutional racism".[1] This recurring brutality forces those on the left to confront the question of how we can end the violence meted out by police.

Brian Bean's *Their End is Our Beginning* traces the origins of the modern US police force as it developed alongside the burgeoning capitalist system. The police, he argues, were created as a means

---

1.   See Coroners Court of the Northern Territory 2025.

of forcing workers to submit to capitalist exploitation. They were professionalised and extended in response to working-class resistance and are used to enforce racial oppression. Bean argues that police violence and racism are not symptoms of the bad attitudes of specific police officers, or even of cultural problems in police organisations. Instead, they're built into the social role of the police. Police forces are not neutral organisations designed to protect ordinary people from crime, but violent institutions whose purpose is to enforce capitalist domination of an oppressed working class. So the police can't simply be reformed or made more culturally sensitive. They must be abolished altogether – a project that rests on the overthrow of capitalism through working-class revolution.

Disciplining the working class

Bean argues that the central role of the police – as the armed wing of the capitalist state – is to dominate and oppress the working class to ensure the flow of profits to the capitalist class. *This argument sets his book apart from mainstream literature* produced on the police, much of which sees police brutality and racist excesses as either accidental or symptomatic of a bad culture which could be transformed through appropriate training. Other authors call for abolition but don't identify the oppressive relationship between the police and the working class. As a result, they look for solutions entirely separate from working-class resistance. For example, settler colonial theory scholar John Kamaal Sunjata argues that "the role of the police has served to protect white supremacy and wealth creation for white people while denying Black people essential human rights".[2] Bean argues that the police do not act for white people in general, but for the capitalist minority. Enforcing the will of this minority necessitates racist brutality.

Capitalists need a domestic armed force to ensure class dominance. Police exist to fulfill this.[3] Under capitalism, workers create value for the rich minority capitalist class but receive only a small amount in return – enough to keep us alive and working. The gap between the value that we create compared to the meagre wage we receive is

2.   Sunjata 2021.
3.   See Lenin 1917.

hoarded by the rich; thus businesses can turn a profit. Workers have a material interest in unravelling capitalism, and the collective power to end it. Bean argues that the modern police were created for the purpose of "the suppression, prevention, and pacification of working-class resistance" (p.13). Police discipline workers who strike or protest and can be mobilised in large numbers to suppress rebellions. Police use force as a means of social control. Because of the constant presence of police on the streets, working-class people know that a toe out of line can mean being arrested.

Police protect the private property of the wealthy, ensuring that workers do not simply reach out and take the goods we have created but instead pay for what we need out of hard-earned wages. As Bean points out, "the motive to steal, rob, trespass, and the like is continually recreated through the pressure of material need" (p.138). Workers are deprived of what they need to live decent lives, creating a pressure towards forms of crime and therefore a need for police intervention. Racism and discipline of other oppressed groups are crucial parts of this project. Deliberate racist oppression of Black people in the United States keeps large swathes of the working-class population in conditions of even more extreme poverty, allows for sections of the class to be paid even lower wages, and helps the state to justify neglect and violence. Racist division breaks up working-class unity, weakening resistance.

The capitalist state, of which the police form part, is a tool of class domination, not a neutral institution. The capitalist state encompasses, in all countries, a sprawling set of institutions which govern over society in the broad interests of the capitalist class. Rather than acting for individual capitalists, the state's role is to advance the interests of the capitalist class in general and to ensure its dominance over the working masses. It includes a political wing, sometimes elected, alongside swathes of unelected bureaucracies which facilitate trade, use of water and land, industrial relations, banking and other aspects of society. The police force and the military are the two key parts of the capitalist state, because they ensure its ability to use armed force over the working class domestically and advance the interests of the ruling class it represents abroad. As Bean argues, "rather than capitalist states being sites of struggle that can be perhaps repurposed for our aims, states are the chief obstacle to achieving abolition" (p.9). To end police oppression, we need to overthrow the capitalist state in its entirety.

Origins of the police

In every form of class society, the ruling class has wielded a violent apparatus to dominate those they exploit. In feudal England, owners of large estates controlled private militias, and the aristocracy used the military to put down rebellions. Modern police originated with the advent of capitalist society. Bean briefly charts the development of the modern working class in Europe. Peasants and the poor were rounded up and forced into immense cities where they were worked to death in factories, living in desperately poor conditions. But, "by assembling them all in one place and forcing them to cooperate on the job, employers also increased the capacity for collective working-class struggle against exploitation and tyranny" (p.59). From its advent, the working class collectively resisted. In doing so, they came into physical conflict with armed representatives of the capitalist class. One example is the Peterloo Massacre. In 1819, workers in Manchester organised themselves in hunger marches, strikes and an illegal union, culminating in 100,000 workers marching on St. Peter's Field on 18 August in military-like columns. Bosses' militias were backed up by the English army, which charged the workers, killed 14 and injured more than 400, provoking bitter riots and working-class organising.

In response to growing working-class resistance, Home Secretary Sir Robert Peel established the London Metropolitan Police force on 29 September 1829. Other nations followed the example. England's Royal Irish Constabulary, used to enforce colonial order in Ireland, became the model for state discipline in European colonial projects including Palestine, India, Egypt and Brazil. In Japan, where the Meiji Restoration ushered in capitalist industrialisation, a combination of the English and the more military-style French policing models was implemented in 1874 after Superintendent General Kawaji Toshiwoshi toured Europe to find a model that would work for the new capitalist state.

The working class did not readily accept the discipline of the cops. Less than two months after the advent of the London Metropolitan

Police, demonstrators converged on parliament house in protest. In Manchester, early police were regularly beaten and in Birmingham a public assembly declared them "a bullying and unconstitutional force" as street fighting pitted workers against cops.

North America

Modern police forces were established in Boston in 1838, New York in 1844 and Chicago in 1853. These were modelled, Bean explains, explicitly on the London Metropolitan Police. At this time bosses hired private security gangs to use against workers, the most famous being the Pinkertons. They infiltrated unions and forcibly broke strikes from the 1850s onward. The rich also relied on semi-private police forces like the Coal and Iron Police, set up by the state government of Pennsylvania but paid for by coal companies to break strikes, evict workers from their homes and protect the property of the coal bosses.[4]

While these private gangs were widely and violently used against workers, Bean argues that "the ruling class, while keen to throw money at private security, much preferred that the forces of repression be socialized, for the reason of cost and the ideological function of their appearing 'public'" (p.66). State-run police forces play an almost identical role to these private firms, but the fact that they're paid for with taxes and work for the government creates an appearance of serving the people. The Pennsylvania State Constabulary, on which the majority of state police forces were modelled, was introduced in response to the 1902 anthracite coal strike in eastern Pennsylvania.

Earlier precursors to American police were the patrols which controlled the enslaved population and disciplined poor and indentured whites, as well as militias like the Texas Rangers which massacred native Americans. The structures and legal codes which governed the lives and discipline of slaves were based on legal codes developed in England to govern the new working class. Bean argues that "the violent construction of the European proletariat and the obscenity of African chattel slavery were tightly bound together" (p. 36). Slaves bravely resisted, and slave owners established armed bands to hunt down men

---

4.   Meyerhuber 1987, pp.37, 76.

and women seeking freedom. Patrols were initially paid for by plantation owners, staffed in particular by property owners, and armed by the white participants themselves. But as they became more stable features of an oppressive society, the patrols were increasingly formalised and taken over by local courts.

Bean introduces a less discussed history of the organisation of slave catching: the inconsistency of participation by poor and indentured whites in slave patrols, and the potential for interracial solidarity. Authorities attempted to mobilise all whites to participate in slave-catching gangs, including poor whites and those in servitude. They hoped that the racist legal systems and social structure would bind the poor to their own race, and used financial incentives to mobilise them to catch slaves. But the poor were unreliable. In 1775, one South Carolina regiment commander complained that "the slave patrols had 'stagnated' because working-class whites were lax in their participation" (p.39). In response, an influx of professional troops bolstered the patrols. Slave owners imposed a punishment of five years of slavery upon any white accomplice to an escaping slave. A Virginia law for the brutal suppression of resistance by the enslaved warned that "dangerous consequences may arise to the country if other negroes, Indians, or [white] servants should happen to fly forth and joyne with them" (p.37).

Discipline, racism and poverty

Today, police forces are far more vast, professional and heavily armed. Since the 1980s, a capitalist offensive against the working class in the United States and Australia has increased police powers and numbers while curtailing access to welfare and social supports.[5] Union rights have come under attack, in tandem with a legal offensive against protesters. At the same time, police numbers in impoverished and racially oppressed communities have ramped up and prison populations have swelled. This has accompanied a neoliberal offensive on the welfare state, with privatisation of services, depletion of bulk billing, and constrained access to dole payments.[6] Sapping funding to social

5. Bramble 2019.
6. Bramble 2014.

services while increasing police spending is sometimes presented as a simple either/or decision that governments are making about budget lines. But police expansion over the last forty years has been, for the capitalist class, a necessary component of their project of constraining social spending and increasing exploitation of the working class.

Police discipline workers in the ruins left behind by decades of attack on living standards. Law and order campaigns are used as an ideological tool to turn working-class people against each other, explaining social decay as a by-product of individual criminality rather than a deliberate choice emerging from attacks upon working-class living standards. Law and order narratives tend to be deeply racialised, both in Australia and in the United States, as is policing itself. For example, Aboriginal people were 4.5 times more likely to receive a COVID-related fine from police than is proportionate to their population in the first half of 2020, while for Sudanese and South Sudanese people the figure was a staggering 35.6 times.[7] This can be traced, in part, to the systematic oppression of both of these groups, including the child removals of the Stolen Generations, the violent forcible removal of Indigenous people from their land and the withholding of basic rights from those who arrive in this country as refugees. It is also rooted in the present-day neglect of these communities. Bean argues, speaking about the United States, that "the organized abandonment of working-class Black neighborhoods is enacted through the economic violence of budget cuts, political disenfranchisement, lack of investment resulting in job scarcity, and entrenched workplace and housing discrimination" (p.144). Much of this is also applicable to impoverished and racially oppressed areas of Australia. But racist policing is also clearly connected to the ideological racism which positions these groups as more prone to criminality, and higher imprisonment rates in turn feed this narrative.

As services and infrastructure come under attack, prisons balloon. In the US, hulking new prisons have been constructed on the barren lands of former mines, sold to impoverished working-class communities with the promise of new jobs and constraint of

---

7.   Hopkins and Popovic 2023.

criminality.[8] In Australia, prisons are increasingly constructed on urban peripheries with high unemployment, and promoted as creating jobs.[9] Governments do not spend on policing and prisons in order to decrease crime rates, but because building up the disciplinary arm of the state is vital to their project of attacking working-class living standards. Impoverished neighbourhoods are told that an increased police presence will protect them, when in reality the purpose of that police presence is to discipline them into accepting their lot.

The way forward

Bean argues, rightly, that the only way to do away with the police is to overthrow capitalism through working-class revolution. Years of "reforms" to United States police departments have led to the brutality we see today. As Alex S Vitale points out in *The End of Policing*, training packages miss the point. Police do not murder Black people because they haven't been trained in appropriate arrest strategies. They do it because the experience of disciplining ordinary people day in and day out teaches police to treat the lives of those they are oppressing with complete disregard. This applies doubly to those who are racially oppressed. Cultural sensitivity training is meaningless when we consider that racism is not a product of individual ideas but a tool used to structure capitalist society, and that police are the armed enforcers of oppression. Attempts to improve policing by recruiting more officers from racially oppressed groups are fraught. Vitale points out that

> there is now a large body of evidence measuring whether the race of individual officers affects their use of force. Most studies show no effect. More distressingly, a few indicate that Black officers are more likely to use force or make arrests, especially of Black civilians.[10]

---

8.   Story 2019, pp.80–82.
9.   For instance, Victoria's Western Plains Correctional Centre opened on 1 July 2025 at a cost of around $1.1 billion: Corrections Victoria 2025. See also Russell et al 2025.
10. Vitale 2017, pp.10–14.

As Bean reminds us, one of the cops who held George Floyd down while Derek Chauvin murdered him was Black.

The Black Lives Matter urban rebellion popularised calls to "abolish" or "defund" police rather than slogans calling only for reform. This was a step forward. These demands alone, however, are insufficient. Bean also advocates for "demands that can reduce the scope, power, and legitimacy of the police state" (p.231). In Australia, this includes demands to end the practice of "designated zones" in working-class areas, ban strip searches, and introduce independent bodies to investigate police brutality and racism rather than allowing police to do it themselves.

Moments of revolution and uprising can also push the oppressed into direct confrontations with the police. Egyptian revolutionary Hossam el-Hamalawy described how at the National Police Day protest during the 2011–12 Egyptian revolution, "when the cops were run off the streets they literally stripped off their uniforms on the spot and sprinted home in their boxers" (p.189).

Ultimately, however, the rule of the capitalists and their police lackeys will always reassert itself if capitalism isn't completely replaced by a socialist system. Police are an essential component of capitalist enforcement, and as long as the system stands it will rely on police violence. So those who want to see the abolition of the police must be for the overthrow of capitalist society altogether, as Bean argues.

Only the working class has the power to overthrow capitalism, because the capitalists directly rely on workers to create the profits that give their class life. By halting production, creating new democratic institutions of worker rule, and carrying out an insurrection to defeat the capitalist state, workers can subordinate the capitalist class and begin the project of creating a socialist society.

To do this, conscious intervention by revolutionary socialist political parties is necessary. In the course of every revolution, an array of political parties and institutions attempt to hold back or crush the advancing working class. A party is necessary to cohere large layers of workers with different ideas, win them to the revolutionary overthrow of capitalism, and organise them in action. Without this, defeat is inevitable. While Bean makes a considered argument for the necessity of revolution, he only briefly mentions the need for a party. This is the key task facing socialists the world over today, including in the United States. In the last twenty years, mass uprisings and revolutions have shaken capitalist countries including Egypt, Sudan, Syria, Lebanon, Hong Kong, Myanmar, Ecuador and others. In every one of these, socialists were unable to take the struggle forward because they lacked the organised forces necessary. Like its counterparts across the world, the American working class is exploited, oppressed, and will at some stage enter into struggle. The key task then, for those who dream of the end of the police and a non-capitalist world, is to begin organising revolutionary forces today.

References

Bramble, Tom 2014, "Australian capitalism in the neoliberal age", *Marxist Left Review*, 7, Summer. https://marxistleftreview.org/articles/australian-capitalism-in-the-neoliberal-age/

Bramble, Tom 2019, "Police state: The politics of law and order", *Marxist Left Review*, 17, Summer. https://marxistleftreview.org/articles/police-state-the-politics-of-law-and-order/

Corrections Victoria 2025, "Western Plains Correctional Centre is ready for opening", 27 June. https://www.corrections.vic.gov.au/about-the-corrections-system/stories-and-statements/western-plains-correctional-centre-opening

Coroners Court of the Northern Territory 2025, *Inquest into the death of Kumanjayi Walker*, NTLC 8, 7 July. https://agd.nt.gov.au/__data/assets/pdf_file/0009/1541754/A00512019-K.-Walker-findings.pdf

Hopkins, Tamar and Gordana Popovic 2023, *Policing COVID-19 in Victoria: exploring the impact of perceived race in the issuing of COVID-19 fines during 2020*, Inner Melbourne Community Legal. https://imcl.org.au/assets/downloads/2304_IMCL_PAP_AA_V2.pdf

Lenin, Vladimir 1917, "They Have Forgotten the Main Thing", *Pravda*, 18 May. https://www.marxists.org/archive/lenin/works/1917/may/05b.htm

Meyerhuber, Carl I 1987, *Less than Forever: the Rise and Decline of Union Solidarity in Western Pennsylvania, 1914–1948*, Selinsgrove: Susquehanna University Press.

Russell, Emma, Andrew Burridge, Francis Markham, Naama Blatman and Natalie Osborne 2025, "Prisons don't create safer communities, so why is Australia spending billions on building them?", *The Conversation*, 23 January. https://theconversation.com/prisons-dont-create-safer-communities-so-why-is-australia-spending-billions-on-building-them-247238

Story, Brett 2019, *Prison Land: Mapping Carceral Power across Neoliberal America*, University of Minnesota Press.

Sunjata, John Kamaal 2021, *On Police Abolition: Decolonization Is The Only Way*, Hampton Institute. https://www.hamptonthink.org/read/on-police-abolition-decolonization-is-the-only-way

Vitale, Alex S 2017, *The End of Policing*, Verso.

www.ingramcontent.com/pod-product-compliance
Lightning Source LLC
Chambersburg PA
CBHW070109030426
42335CB00016B/2079